ENCOUNTER WITH SOCIOLOGY: The Term Paper
Second Edition

ENCOUNTER WITH SOCIOLOGY:

The Term Paper

Second Edition

Leonard Becker Jr.
John F. Kennedy University

and Clair Gustafson
Diablo Valley College

Boyd & Fraser Publishing Company — San Francisco

Leonard Becker, Jr. and Clair Gustafson

ENCOUNTER WITH SOCIOLOGY: THE TERM PAPER
Second Edition

Copyright © 1976 by Boyd & Fraser Publishing Company.

Library of Congress Catalog Card Number 76-8791

International Standard Book Number 0-87835-056-x

1 2 3 4—9 8 7 6

Acknowledgements

Among those who helped with the first edition, we would once again like to give special thanks to Sharon Swigert and Neal Hansen, who helped put the book together, and to Tate Davie, Sharon Hanson, Christine Heller, Pete Lowenberg, David Morris, Claire Schulberg, and Sally Todd, who allowed us to excerpt from term papers written in Donald A. Hansen's introductory sociology class at the University of California, Santa Barbara.

We wish to thank the professors and students who recommended the first edition and suggested a second. Kichi Iwamoto of the Department of Sociology at the University of Santa Clara made a number of cogent suggestions that we incorporated into the revision. We also appreciate the editorial work of Victoria Nelson, and the help of Caryn Iwamoto and Valerie Lacy in research and typing.

Last, but most important, we thank those closest to us, who have accommodated to the irregular interruptions of the work.

LB

CG

BERKELEY
JANUARY 1976

Preface

We designed the first edition of *Encounter with Sociology* primarily for first-year college students interested in learning about sociology by a means beyond lectures, discussions, and reading assignments. We also had in mind professors of sociology who would be interested in seeing students begin to do exploratory research, even if such attempts would be quite tentative and remote from their professional standards.

We assumed that most of the undergraduates who would use *Encounter* were not headed for careers in sociology and would therefore miss first-hand acquaintance with the methods and the discipline unless they were exposed to them in a course that included field work. We also assumed that field work would offer a refreshing contrast to academic abstractions. Therefore we included the traditions of library research and documentation, but emphasized the basics of field research.

To embody these assumptions, we organized the book in two sections. The first was a sixty-six page primer for a one-term research project in the field or in the library. The second was a fifty-seven page set of appendices, which expanded the basics but made no attempt to serve sophisticated researchers. Books that did so were listed at the end of the appropriate chapters and appendices.

The first edition has been used successfully and steadily in a range of courses throughout the social sciences. We believe that this breadth of appeal validates our intention to provide the guidelines for a taste of research, rather than to provide an intensive "introduction" to professional sociology. As one sociologist said, "It takes the student from A to D, rather than from A to Z. And D is as far as most students can possibly go in one term."

The second edition retains the approach and organization of the first. We have rewritten the text to make it clearer and to make it even more practical through detailed examples of choosing the topic, narrowing it, and sharpening the thesis. We have included the citation form of the *American Sociological Review* along with the traditional forms of footnote documentation. (Because even professionals may have trouble with these forms, we stress that the student's fairness, accuracy, and consistency are more important than his or her ability to reproduce one style or the other perfectly.)

We have expanded and brought up-to-date the lists of references and further readings. And we have added material on asking questions, pretesting, constructing tables, and using statistics. Throughout the book we use a familiar, informal style to keep students close to the process that will, we hope, absorb them. We explain, in the chapter on writing the report, that a more formal—but not more deadly—style is best for the term paper. Yet we believe, and try to demonstrate, that involvement with a topic brings it to life; and if the student is alive to the research and writing, that liveliness is well worth some loss in professional precision.

Introduction

Let's be honest. A term paper can be a grueling bore for both you and your reader, especially if it appears as simply another obstacle in an academic steeplechase. The assignment is actually an opportunity to deepen, not deaden, your interest in a subject. No matter how intimidating or dull the prospect may seem at first glance, the assignment is a way of getting you closer to life by a path that may be new to you.

"Term paper" is an ambiguous phrase. It can refer to a paper that covers the main points in a course lasting one term—a quarter, a semester, or even a year. Or it may be a long essay based on armchair analysis of one point from the course. But as assigned in most courses, a term paper is a report based on library or field research, and that is the sense we give it in this book.

The term paper is a process of exploration as well as a product, a report. Good research is always explorative, not mechanical or cut-and-dried. Research should be thoughtfully planned and carefully done, but done with intense curiosity rather than with the sense of rehashing foregone conclusions. If you make the mistake of thinking your work must be definitive and perfect, the assignment will inevitably become tedious. The term paper is, after all, only one part of one course. Give the job reasonable but not undue attention, and the time invested will prove a good return both to you and to your instructor.

The term paper in sociology gives you a chance to use traditional principles of research along with the special methods of sociology. Your purpose is to explore a topic by asking questions based on sociological principles. In the process of answering those questions—or at least of shedding light on them—you discover new angles to the topic and, finally, crystallize your experience and attitudes in a report. In this book, we stress the importance of starting with a topic based on a personal interest. The first chapter suggests ways of choosing a topic based on your experience and interests. The other chapters show how to set realistic limits, outline and carry out the research, analyze the information, and, finally, write up the whole effort so the reader can share some of the adventure along with the data and conclusions.

Because many students find field research more stimulating than library work, we show how to plan and complete sensible questionnaires and interviews as well as how to use the library. Field research is especially good at bringing close the frustration and fascination of applying classroom abstractions to mundane reality. It brings the sociological assumptions and questions to life. As one student in an introductory course testified:

> The value of this paper is not in the actual findings or the scanty interpretations, but in having experienced the social process. This process of personal confrontation gives one hints of the way people are people, and these glimpses are all part of understanding the art of people.

Assuming that most readers of this book will be students in introductory courses, we have condensed the basics of research and report writing into seven short chapters. We hope that even if you were to read all seven at one sitting, they are clear and concise enough to give a stimulating overview of the possibilities and requirements of the project. We believe the chapters are sufficiently detailed to make up a step-by-step guide as well. The several appendices, intended for further reference, expand the basics without cluttering the introductory discussion of these basics. The material in these appendices is included for two reasons: it is useful for introductory level projects but best read for reference, or it is material easily integrated into advanced research. Because the first edition of this book was used in advanced as well as introductory courses, we have expanded, updated, and annotated the lists of references. These include bibliographies of sociological topics, books and articles on research techniques, and term paper guides more detailed than this one.

Introduction

x

We hope this book will help keep you alive and well through the task. Expect problems and pitfalls, especially if you try field work. They are part of research. Resolve them to the best of your ability, but don't hide them when the time comes to write the report. Your instructor expects you to have had difficulties; how you handled these difficulties is an important part of the process. So don't "keep a low profile" or cover up your compromises. Your instructor doesn't expect you to be a machine that simply researches, records, and regurgitates. And don't expect your instructor to be a machine that simply weighs and grades. In fact, he or she may have a special style or set of limits for the work. If so, be sure to note them in the appropriate sections of this book. Then sit back, read, and begin to think your way into your term paper.

Contents

Choosing

a

Topic

First, consider yourself. The best topics come out of your own interest, so choose something to explore in depth that is already a part of your life. This may be an interest you pursue now or one you would like to find out more about. Allow your ideas to flow. Consider several possibilities from several angles. A good topic will strike you as provocative, full of possibilities, and a chance to deepen your knowledge. Start by running through your immediate interests. Some of these may seem trivial, but, as we will show later, nothing is too trivial if developed with an eye to sociological concerns.

You might take a sociological perspective immediately by considering a topic from the point of view of a group. What groups interest you? Look close to home. Families? Fellow students? Students at your old high school? Churchgoers? Shoppers? Football fans? Library users? By staying close to home, you can develop a topic into a practical project for field research. As you think of these groups, remember what you have seen about their behavior, interests, concerns. Suppose you shop at a supermarket but have been in and out of small neighborhood stores. You might wonder if the buying patterns of customers in these "Mom and Pop" stores differ from those of customers who frequent supermarkets. And what about the customers in quick-stop grocery stores? Are they somewhere between the Mom and Pop shoppers and the supermarket customers? The next step would be to run over the aspects of the topic that might be fascinating and practical to explore. Prices. Shelf time. Check cashing. Credit. Knowledge of the customer. Special orders. Background and ambitions of employees. Perhaps you can interview regular customers and employees. The effect is to make your shopping trips a chance to learn as well as to spend.

Another approach is to consider social concerns. These topics are always under investigation and thus are the subject of many scholarly and popular articles. They can be explored either in the library alone or in both the library and the field. Unemployment, prisons, civil liberties, leisure, corporate power, professional sports, violence, sex roles, drugs, student government, political ethics, prostitution—the list is endless, and one way to check it is to consult the subject listing of *Sociological Abstracts*. But before you start to check articles themselves, think through the aspects that already concern you or have been in the news.

Another angle is to think of places where special groups congregate. Parks, concert halls, airports, banks, hospitals, hotels, communes, beaches, clubs, bars, restaurants, offices—even wilderness trails, which nowadays are getting crowded. What about the possibilities of "the city"? A boom in massage parlors? Zoning disputes? Street vendors bucking license laws? Integration of schools? Highly trained professionals joining the ranks of the unemployed? The shift in emphasis among minority males from success in athletics to success in the professions? The ascending ambitions of women athletes—from joining Little Leagues to setting the pace in long-distance events? The rising consciousness of men—their needs beyond working and winning? The new popularity of law school? Community debate over a new traffic plan? Vans, their users and uses? The culture of citizen band radios? Law enforcement issues—demilitarizing police, hiring and use of women officers, strikes? The resurgence of fraternities and sororities?

Each of these broad subjects has many aspects. Viewing a subject from one aspect turns it into a topic. Focusing on one aspect, furthermore, is the only way a subject can become manageable in the limits of a term paper. And as the next chapter explains, sharpening your focus is your next task. This will clarify your research, and improve the quality of your experience. A way to do this is to imagine the subject or group as it affects one person.

Suppose a young man arrives at college and finds himself unfashionably dressed. He might have to resolve a conflict between retaining his "natural" style and adopting the collegiate style. He might have the further problem of choosing among several styles fashionable on the campus—each style perhaps associated with a style of life. Seen in a sociological perspective, his problem becomes one of group identification. The subject is collegiate fashion. The angle here is a male's point of view, with the implication that the situation is a problem requiring the young man to break with some traditions and adopt others. What are some other angles? How does the young man discover he's out of style? Simple observation? Friendly advice? Magazines? Clothing stores? One way to explore the subject, then, would be to find out how students form their opinions about campus dress. Another way would be to find out how the patterns of dress are set. At this point, you can sense that the topics raise not only basic sociological questions about group structure and operation, but also questions of value. Can clothes influence a college man's social life and perhaps his future prospects? Should a young man choose his tie and blazer or boots and Levi's with as much care as, no doubt, he lavishes on choosing his records and books? What are the limits of conformity?

The late sociologist C. Wright Mills has noted that this shift from a "personal trouble" to a "public issue" is the essence of the sociological imagination.

Troubles occur within the character of the individual and within the range of his immediate relations with others; they have to do with his immediate relations with others; they have to do with his self and with those limited areas of social life of which he is directly and personally aware. . . .

Issues have to do with matters that transcend these local environments of the individual and the range of his inner life. . . . An issue, in fact, often involves a crisis in institutional arrangements . . . .

. . . .

What we experience in various and specific milieux, I have noted, is often caused by structural changes. Accordingly, to understand the changes of many personal milieux we are required to look beyond them. . . . To be aware of the idea of social structure and to use it with sensibility is to be capable of tracing such linkages among a great variety of milieux. To be able to do that is to possess the sociological imagination.*

For another example of a topic that comes from a subject by way of a personal interest, suppose you liked to roller skate. Even though this idea seems trivial at first, it is just such a personal interest that can become valuable. How can this be transformed from a personal satisfaction (not a "trouble," in this case) to a public issue? First of all, don't feel you have to make a Big Issue of it to make an apparently trivial concern a worthwhile research topic. "Public concern" means the topic should go beyond a simple description of some group behavior to a discussion of why the topic is worth the reader's (and researcher's) attention. The topic might start from personal curiosity, but somewhere along the line it should develop a larger interest. Before we get too abstract, let's follow a line of thinking:

> Let's see. I like to roller skate. How in the world could that be a paper for Soc? Got my first pair at about 6. Little kids roller skating? A Study of the Effect of Roller Skates on Friendships Among Six- to Ten-Year-Olds in My Neighborhood. Get serious. Used to go to roller rinks in high school. Lots of action there. Definite groups and interesting behavior patterns. Tough groups, middle-class types, minorities, styles of skating, mating rituals, the freedom of the place. Yeah, a little adolescent world, like school but freer and faster. Gangs, fights, dope, the importance of money, cars, skill. Don't go skating much anymore. Not my crowd now. Any place older people skate? How about roller derby? Maybe that's where old skaters keep in touch. But I don't watch. Too rough and lower class. Like wrestling. Ritualized violence. Maybe I

The Sociological Imagination (New York: Oxford University Press, 1959), pp. 8-11.

C h o o s i n g a T o p i c

could do something on roller rinks working into roller derby. Or maybe I could focus on one or the other. I can remember something about roller rinks dying out. And the women derby types—I remember reading about one or two of them. Strange contrasts, especially in light of the women's movement. Women making a good living knocking each other around—real macho stuff. Competence plus violence. How does somebody like that handle the shift to the stock feminine role? Or does she? I could look up the articles on it, check with some rink operators, and maybe interview some derby types if there are any around here. But that woman's angle is remote to me, and it could mean a lot of tracking down. Interesting thought, especially the women's role and the institution of violence angles. But that idea of sticking with the groups at the rink would be interesting too—social groupings, rites of passage, pop culture. Probably not much in the library on it, but maybe I'd be surprised. A good field project—spending all my time at one rink, picking out people to interview and observe. Maybe questionnaires. Maybe I could take some movies and show the class. Or at least stills to illustrate the paper. But I think I'll start with the idea of observing and interviewing skaters—and the rink owner and manager.

These thoughts move from strictly personal associations to social issues. Probing any subject is bound to develop lines of inquiry that will guide both the research and the reader's interest. Let's try one more example, this time following a personal interest in a public issue. Suppose you were interested in the back-to-the-soil movement of young prople frustrated with urban problems and settling on what they hope will be self-sustaining farms.

Been reading about kids getting out of pollution and the swinging ratrace, getting back to living on farms. Hard work, but real work. Independence, simplicity. But thinking people. OK. How to follow up to make it a project? I don't know any such people. Could look up the newspaper and magazine articles. Wonder if any sociologists have written about it. Check with the librarian, maybe the instructor. How could I make it a field project? A pun. How about a title: Fieldwork Among the New Family Farmers? No, seriously. Fieldwork. Where are these fields? Some in the northern part of this state. I suppose in many states. But I could visit some counties on a couple of weekends. Make a good trip. But I'd like to stop into some county offices. They probably have information about who's moved in where. Especially in the small or sparsely settled counties. Probably find county agents that could steer me to just the right new farmers. Interview the farmers, the county agents, who else? What do I want to know?

Note that at this point the thought turns from specific questions to questions that raise issues.

> What brought them out, who they are, how they're doing, how they're getting along with the old residents, how the old residents view the movement, maybe the attitudes of bankers financing the farm equipment. Maybe there's an interest among farm equipment manufacturers in re-issuing tools and machinery outmoded by large-scale farming. Getting carried away.

Now the thinker gets "carried away" into forming tentative assumptions, a natural and interesting step.

> Wonder if the movement is a delayed disaster—the new farmers headed for bankruptcy and despair. Or maybe it's revitalizing rural areas that decayed when large-scale farming changed the economy of farming. How about federal and state aid? Aimed at large-scale farms? Those who have, get? (The rich get richer, the poor get poorer?) Big issues, all right. But back to the weekend trips. County offices will be closed. Maybe I could make a few phone calls or write letters to get the lay of the land, then take a work vacation—a day or two off of school. Have to set things up carefully so as not to waste the time.

Even if you don't think in just this style, the idea is to pick a subject that interests you, probe it, and focus on one aspect of it. Note in these examples how the practical questions of research guided the ideas. You can begin to see the need for developing a well thought-out plan for finding and questioning the group you are studying. If you stroll in with the vague notion of "getting the feel of things" through the first interviews, the result might be wasted time and mushy, diffuse information. As you begin to narrow the topic and develop a thesis, your project will come into even sharper focus. The sharper the focus, the more productive your time.

Narrowing

the

Topic

The next step is to narrow the topic. Narrowing means tightening the focus and clarifying the limits of the topic so that it fits the limits of the assignment, the scope of possible resources, and the range of your abilities. Don't think of narrowing as trivializing. It is a necessary step in any research project because it enables the researcher to give depth to the questions and methods of the investigation. Trying to cover a broad topic, especially in an introductory course, guarantees shallow, misleading research in both the library and the field.

For example, a year or two and at least 500 pages would be necessary to make this student's topic feasible:

> I wish to examine the sociological, psychological, physiological, and moral issues involved in considering the liberalizing of American laws on the medical termination of a pregnancy.

Covering this topic in, say, 3,000 words would mean either stretching a little information transparently thin or compressing good research into a dense, opaque lump. If an instructor assigned you a vast topic to cover in a general survey, the resulting shallowness would be a built-in limitation of the assignment. If in doubt about the limits, ask. If you're too shy or too stubborn to ask, choose to explore narrowly and deeply.

Narrowing means asking two basic questions: 1) What are my assumptions about this topic? and 2) What could I do to test these assumptions? These questions and your answers interweave in a give-and-take process of clarifying both what you would like to check out and how this checking out could be done. In the last chapter we showed the process beginning to develop, so let's go back to the beginning again and carry the topic through from choosing to narrowing, ending with an essential one- or two-sentence statement of the project.

Let's start from scratch with a random example. Imagine another student staring into space, thinking. Also imagine one taking notes on the best leads. (Jotting phrases or sentences is important, as it means you have a record of all those good ideas. Otherwise you wake up the next morning wondering just what it was that sent you to bed so sure you had a topic. One caution: don't abbreviate. It's maddening to check your notes the next morning and wonder if "j.d." meant "juvenile delinquency" or "jury duty" or "justice division.")

> Let's see. A topic. Maybe close to home. My family? Nothing too interesting there. Work and play. Uncle Mort likes to play cards. Likes to gamble. Gambling. He's a gambler. Not a professional. Professional gambling? Weekend gamblers? Poker players. Horse race addicts. Yeah, gambling is kind of romantic. I've never seen Mort more alive than when he's looking forward to a horse race, a bowl game, a poker game. Maybe "the romance of gambling." Lots of movies and stories. What about research? Talk to Mort and his buddies. Maybe a little too close to home.

Narrowing the Topic

At this point the student shifts from a personal to a public point of view. Note the trial and error nature of the exploration. Don't be afraid to poke around, to discover blind alleys, to free associate.

> Must be a lot on it in the library. Scholarly articles? Must be some sociologists who have looked into the phenomenon. Lots of interest in state lotteries. Some gambling is legal because of skill—horse racing and poker. Legal gambling in Las Vegas. Mafia ties to gambling. Good library paper, at least lots of popular articles. Complex subject. Why so much money in gambling business? People seem driven to gamble. A disease? People do it whether legal or illegal. Need it. Must be a difference between why people say they gamble and why a psychologist would say they do. Sounds too hard to get to the real reasons behind the stated reasons. What kind of gambling might be easy to study but still be interesting? Strange gambling. Betting. Numbers running in New York. Could do a library paper on that—at least see what's been written on the numbers way of life. Poor people looking for a release from grinding routine. The sweepstakes. More middle class, maybe. Who are the winners of the Irish Sweepstakes? How does winning affect their lives? Another library paper. Can't seem to get out of the library. Do I want to? Need a cup of coffee.

If you find yourself getting in a rut, take a break, walk around, get your mind off of it for half an hour or so. Sometimes letting the topic simmer for a day or so will mean new ideas when you return to focusing on it. Sometimes talking it over with a friend will inspire you.

> Maybe I could interview a winner if there's been one around here. Could call the local sports editor. He must know a lot about gambling on sports. What kind of sports? Usual—football, horse racing. A sport? Of kings. Range of horse-race addicts. Must be some studies of the different social groups at the races. Winner's circle—rich owners, the patron's box, like a box at the opera. Stable owners to stable boys. Jockeys have a world of their own. Carson McCuller's story "The Jockey." One by Hemingway, too. "My Old Man." The jockey as a way of life. Library research plus maybe some interviews with jockeys. Remember news stories on women jockeys. Also on fixing of races—organized crime.
>
> So far, best bets are social groups at the track. If that's too general from what I see in the articles, maybe I could choose one group—jockeys or owners or very poor people or bookies or the people who just

hang around the track. Possibility of spending some time at the race-track nearby—if it's racing season. If it's not, maybe interview who-ever is around in management or even among workers. If I did jockeys, maybe I could send a questionnaire to a sample from a list I could get from some jockeys' association. Maybe I could start the paper with some references to the image of jockeys in movies and literature. Could look up scholarly stuff on horse racing, gambling, jockeys. Popular stuff on jockeys. Maybe interview sportswriter who covers racing—good tips from him. He might take me to a race. Uncle Mort and me. Maybe I could do a little betting after talking to jockeys. Might work that into the report. College student does research, gets rich quick. Wonder if I could deduct any losses from my income tax. Is being a student a business? What do jockeys deduct as business ex-penses? Wonder if they do any betting on the horses.

OK—time to get down to it. Narrow. Focus. State in a sentence or two. "I'm going to work on the topic of jockeys—find out their way of life by doing library research and maybe a questionnaire or some interviews." Tighten that. "My topic is the way of life of jockeys in American horse racing." Hmm. Wonder if some of them race at tracks all around the world or if they stick close to home. "My topic is the special life of the American jockey. My method of investigation will be primarily library research with the possibility of a questionnaire sent to a sample of jockeys, and interviews with jockeys at the local track." That leaves plenty of openings.

Start with a little library work. After reading there, I'll feel good about calling someone up at the newspaper and maybe going to talk with whoever covers horse racing. Could talk to Mort, but now is probably not the right time. Get more background so he doesn't give me bum steers. And if we go to the track together, I'll know what to look for. Wonder how I might arrange interviews with the jockeys. Maybe the sportswriter can give me tips—or at least I can talk to the management of the track. But first a couple of days in the library.

We hope this example of the narrowing process gives you ideas about following your own thoughts in provocative directions. Note that this student ended by focusing on jockeys after starting with his family, his uncle, and gambling. Jockeys emerge in his thinking because they are a group connected to gambling through racing and are a group that the student thinks will also have attracted scholars. For research methods, the library is the obvious starting point. The fieldwork comes to the student as a handy way of clarifying impres-sions. The most difficult approach he considers would be the ques-tionnaire mailed to a sample of jockeys. The return from such a questionnaire would no doubt be small and thus frustrating, if that method were the student's main effort. But in this case the student starts realistically—a preliminary talk with the local horse race reporter. If interviews with jockeys or responses to questionnaires prove difficult to get, the research can become a solid library effort embellished by a talk with the local news reporter.

For an example that is perhaps closer to home, imagine a student considering the broad topic of "college life."

> What interests me most about life around here? The chance to meet new people. How do I meet new people? How does anyone around here meet new people? I want to get out of the old high school clique. Some people around here are far from home, so they have to meet new people. Others are commuters like me. I've met a couple of interesting people in the car pool. Do something on car pools? Doesn't really interest me. Ways to meet people. Join a fraternity or sorority. Join a club. Hang out at the hang-outs. Say hello to people in classes. Go to parties. Dull. What's a unique way of meeting people? Well, doing this paper might be one way.
>
> What people do I want to meet through this project? Who do I want to interview? Who are some interesting people in my classes? Alfredo. From Africa. Foreign student. How about how foreign students relate to natives—and to each other. Sounds easy, and something that would give me a chance to meet people I'd never talk to otherwise. How come I haven't met them? Nothing on campus I've noticed gets me involved with them. Wonder how they chose this campus? Maybe they have to have local sponsors. Relatives and friends already in the community. Maybe they don't look to the campus for their relationships. Do they come in pairs? No, that's crazy.
>
> OK. "My topic is the way foreign students relate with each other and with native students. My method of research will be to interview a sample of foreign students." Wonder if the number is small enough so I could interview all of them. Or at least give each of them a questionnaire and collect it. How about a questionnaire for native students asking them if they know foreign students, if they've had any contact with them, if they have any interest, or if they're completely ignorant or unconcerned about the idea that foreign students might want to make friends here but haven't the opportunities? Maybe that's getting too broad.
>
> Focus on finding out, from someone in the registrar's office, how many foreign students are enrolled, how I can get in touch with them, and anything else. Maybe there are programs for foreign students. Then I could talk with the program directors. Maybe they have a foreign stu-

dents' club. They may be interested in getting in touch with more of
their own through my efforts. To the registrar, then the dean of students
or some such office, to find out about a club or organization. Should
give some thought to the kind of questions I'll be interested in. Vital
facts—age, sex, country, time in U. S., time on this campus, major,
work status, plans for study here, plans on completion of studies, career
goals, living arrangement here, finances—could be touchy, maybe a
chart of people they know well, know slightly, knew already, the people at work, in classes, etc.

Point is, who do they know, how did they get to know them, what
are their interests, would they like to know more people? Open-ended
kind of interview. Maybe a talk with two or three will give me more
specific information to make up my final set of questions. Should be
careful about getting too much from one or two people—or relying on
it. Should also talk with school officials about their ideas on the topic.

OK. Summarize. "My topic is the interaction of foreign students
with each other and with the native students. My purpose is to find out
the local ties of foreign students, how they formed them, and what fur-
their ties they might want. The method will be interviews with foreign
students and with school officials involved with foreign students, with
possibly a questionnaire." What about the library? Should check sociological and other sources under "foreign students." Probably a terrific
amount of popular articles on the subject—maybe even a foreign students' newsletter or journal. Check the sociological sources and education journals first to see if any specialized work done. Then some popular articles to get the outlines clear. Then some talks with Alfredo and
others. Or maybe talk over my plan with Alfredo and get some direction. Yeah, start there.

Starting with the idea of college life, this student weaves a personal
interest into the project so that it is likely to become much more than
just another academic obstacle.

What are other directions for considering college life? Living
arrangements, leisure activities, study patterns, health problems,
finances, work patterns, sports, politics, and so forth. Suppose your
campus has some innovation—a new theater, a new department, co-ed
dorms, a campus in another country. You may want to explore the
basic questions of who uses it, why, what happens. For example, what
happens when students live in a co-ed dorm?

Clarifying and limiting means asking more questions. What happenings do you have in mind? Dorms just at your campus, or the co-ed
dorm movement as a whole? Maybe you start with a popular concern

Narrowing the Topic

and work deeper. Does living in a co-ed dorm affect sexual activity? Does it increase mental stress? Does it affect friendship patterns? Marriage patterns?

Suppose you chose marriage patterns, a long-range question. Another question would then be: What do you mean by "affect"? That the marriages will last longer than marriages among those living in segregated dorms? That co-ed residents marry sooner than segregated residents? That the marriages show different patterns than others?

As you can see, a long-range question raises tough but not impossible limitations. You can't wait for residents to get married, so you have to see what's happened to past residents. If co-ed dorms came to your campus a year ago, you could check for marriages, and perhaps engagements, during that year. But there would probably be so few that your study would be futile. The next step would be to compare *attitudes* toward marriage—to see if co-ed residents had changed their attitudes since moving in, or to see if attitudes differed from those held by segregated residents.

If co-ed dorms had been established four or five years ago, "future" questions might be answered by studying the marriage patterns of ex-residents. Suppose the question became specific: Will students in co-ed dorms be more likely to marry one of their co-residents than a resident from outside the dorm? You could then look for married ex-residents through the alumni association, present dorm residents, the dorm staff, and a sample of ex-residents (by questionnaire). The practical considerations show that the topic is a tough one for field research. But the working out of such a project, including a stint in the library, can be an interesting, effective term paper even if the data turn out to be sketchy and your conclusions therefore tentative. The project is still a reasonable effort that will teach you the elements of defining and collecting relevant information.

In considering these possibilities, don't forget basic definitions. What is a co-ed dorm? The answer may seem so obvious as to go without saying—or thinking through. But some dorms alternate floors to separate the sexes while housing them in the same building. Others have segregated wings with a common lounge and dining room. Others alternate rooms, so the sexes share elevators, bathrooms, and bedroom walls. Some dorms are run entirely by undergraduates, some have graduate students as staff, some have a combination of professionals and students, and some have strictly professional management.

As you narrow, define, and clarify, watch for any "drift" in your topic. If it starts out as "sexual behavior of dorm residents" and gradually becomes "the attitudes of dorm residents about sex," be aware of the shift. Changing the topic is fine as long as you know where you're going. Otherwise your assumptions will misdirect your research. A questionnaire that asks about attitudes can say nothing about behavior. It can be made to include information on both attitudes and behavior as long as you have an idea about how to connect the two sets of answers. But if you don't think through your assumptions on the links between behavior and attitudes, the questions will lack fundamental connection and thus the answers will resist integration.

The basic questions to help definition are: 1) Who are the people involved in your inquiry? and 2) What specific information do you want to find out from them? A good idea is to list the characteristics that identify these people and the information you expect from them. For example, for the study on marriage among co-ed dorm residents, the essential requirement might be: A resident for at least one semester in a co-ed dorm between (appropriate dates) who married after having lived in the dorm. The information to be collected might include sex; age; present marital status; if married, whether spouse was a resident of the same dorm; attitudes about marriage before and after dorm experience.

For a last example stressing definition, let's look again at the tough one that started this chapter.

> I wish to examine the sociological, psychological, physiological, and
> moral issues involved in considering the liberalizing of American laws
> on the medical termination of a pregnancy.

Note that the student already has narrowed the topic considerably by specifying the issues, the idea of liberalizing, the laws only in America, and abortion only by doctors. To narrow further, we could keep the same number of issues and restrict the group, or we could use the same group but restrict the issues. Or we could go both ways, narrowing both the issues and the group: "Is there any connection between physiological and moral issues in the minds of obstetricians regarding the liberalizing of California laws on abortion?" It could be even narrower: "How do the thirty obstetricians practicing in Siesta City, California, define 'a human life,' and how do these definitions influence their attitudes toward the liberalizing of California laws on abortion? Do these definitions rest on scientific or religious principles?''

Now to explain how we develop these restrictions. The first question is of course "How can the topic be covered in one term?" The next question is also basic: "Why should anyone care about the topic, the liberalizing of abortion laws?" That question directly points up the interest of several groups, such as mothers with "too many" children, parents worried about a disastrous combining of their incompatible heredities, lawyers who may have to prosecute to defend abortionists, legislators who may have a vote on the proposed changes, and doctors who may have to advise parents and actually perform abortions. "Doctors" is a good choice because they operate as well as contemplate. "Would some doctors be more involved than others and thus have more significant opinions?" General practitioners, perhaps, as they often are a family's general advisor and can perform abortions. "What about pediatricians, who may be influenced by treating children with birth defects?" "Obstetricians" is probably better because they specialize in pregnancy and birth and also perform abortions as a regular part of their practice.

A few more questions reveal even richer possibilities. "Does 'obstetrician' mean 'licensed and practicing'?" If so, doctors in obstetrical residency and retired obstetricians don't qualify. Eliminating them reduces the time necessary to gather information; but that gain must be weighed against the loss of a possibly significant body of information and opinion. Residents will soon become perhaps outspoken voices in their profession, and retired obstetricians have experience and reputation behind their beliefs. "What about professors of obstetrics who teach but don't practice?" They write articles read by the practitioners and thus may have a real influence on at least the physiological issue of defining "a human life." But enough is enough. Too many questions all at once can kill a topic, and if it dies for you, it will deaden your reader. More often, though, the clarifying and narrowing bring the topic to life. Your imagination blends theoretical and practical concerns into a topic that really becomes your own.

Thesis
and
Hypotheses

Chapter Three

We hope by now you're clear on some of the ways a topic moves from a general interest, like gambling, to a focus, such as American jockeys. We also hope you have some sense of the appropriate research—in this case, library research plus interviews with jockeys, a sportswriter, and an official of a racetrack. The next step toward setting up the project is to devise a *thesis*. A thesis is simply a concise statement of your central belief about the topic. For example, the topic of this book is obviously "basic guidelines for term papers in sociology." The thesis is: "College students need guidelines for term papers in sociology." A more complex thesis is: "Though students can gather and report information, they need assistance in applying their skills to the term paper in sociology." A thesis is a response to the question: What is your central belief about the topic? The more specific the answer, the more defined the project and the more clear-cut the path of research. In stating a thesis, you take a position. The best position is not only the one you believe but also the one most worthwhile investigating in the limited time available.

After the narrowing process, you can form a preliminary thesis without research. If necessary, you can adjust, revise, or reject this thesis during the first stages of your research. But eventually, before research begins in earnest, you must devise a thesis that your research can support or disprove. Let's take the topic "American jockey" through its development into some theses:

How would I form a thesis for my ideas on jockeys? What are some of these ideas? That jockeys stick together on and off the track, maybe because of their specialized occupation, maybe because of their having to travel a lot, maybe because of their size. They probably live it up when they're winning or maybe between race seasons. They must have to take care of themselves carefully, especially their weight and reflexes. Probably no drinking. Wonder if they drug themselves up before a race. Wonder what the pattern of getting ready for a race is. How do they move up through the ranks? Do they have to have influence among horse owners? Do they have to curry favor? Do they believe in the horses they ride—have favorites? Do they bet on races—on themselves? Against the rules? Break the rules if there are some? What's the code of ethics? Brings me back to gambling. That could be a way of tying into my original interest. Let's see. How does a jockey's life interact with the gambling around the racing? Should be a better statement. Does the jockey have to separate his professional efforts and private life from the gambling aspect of horse-racing? OK, make a definite statement. "My thesis is that jockeys keep their professional and private lives immune from the gambling around horseracing." What does that mean? A jockey cannot afford to gamble on races. How about another thesis? "American professional jockeys don't bet or directly cooperate with bettors on horseraces."

Note that the effort of forming a thesis further clarifies the topic. Moreover, it points the way toward defining specific questions that will, when answered, take you further into the narrowing process.

Consider again the topic of jockeys and betting. The principle thesis for library work would be: "Articles about jockeys will either state that jockeys stay away from horse race betting or they will make no mention of jockeys and betting." This thesis leads to another question: Are jockeys punished either by state law or professional associations for betting on horse races? One thesis would be: "Jockeys are prohibited by law from betting on horse races and infractions are taken seriously." Another would be: "Professional associations severely punish jockeys who bet on horseraces." Three theses for field research might be: 1) "jockeys deny involvement with the betting around horse races;" 2) "racetrack officials believe jockeys stay clear of betting;" and 3) "sportswriters covering horse racing believe jockeys stay clear of betting."

To show the importance to the research of a clear thesis, consider the topic "student drinking." We could narrow the topic to "a drinking problem among the students." This leads to a question, and the answer leads to a thesis:

Question: Is there a drinking problem among students at this college?

Thesis: There is a drinking problem among students at this college.

The thesis is a statement of belief. The opposite belief gives the opposite thesis: There is no drinking problem on campus. The next step is to sharpen the thesis, which means thinking of ways to identify what we mean by "drinking problem." If a problem for the campus, we would be looking for confirmation from campus officials, including deans and the police. If we see it as a personal problem, we would look to the students for data. If we believe it to be an official problem, we could restate the thesis more precisely: "Campus officials consider drinking among students a problem." That thesis suggests any drinking among students is a problem. Could we do better? "Excessive drinking among students is a campus problem." That thesis points to an investigation of the concepts "excessive drinking" and "campus problem."

Now we can take the next step. The first source would be the office of the dean of students. If such a problem exists, the evidence in all likelihood would be there. Thesis: "Campus officials, such as the dean of students, define excessive drinking among students as a problem." In the course of talking with such officials, we would be alert to what they identify as the problem. Parental complaints?

Thesis and Hypotheses

Complaints from off-campus residents? Vandalism? Absenteeism? Illegality? Nuisances? Complaints from other students? From instructors? Poor grades among drinkers? It would be important to discover frequencies, some kind of objective data. How many students are dismissed each term with excessive drinking given as a major cause? How many complaints a month come from dorm supervisors? How often are campus police needed to handle a drunken party? What does drunken vandalism cause in dollar damages?

Sometimes the official perspective on a problem needs to be complemented by another approach. Who else might have experience with excessive drinking among students? One group would be the students themselves. Thesis: "It is common knowledge among students that excessive drinking is a campus problem." The term "common knowledge" suggests that any reasonable sample of students will turn up evidence for the problem. If that isn't our belief, we have to think through to the students who might have that knowledge. What students would know about drinking? Thesis: "Students in positions of responsibility, like dorm counselors, student government officers, fraternity and sorority presidents, and any students who work or live around places where drinking problems come to light—bars, movie theaters, restaurants, bus terminals, stadiums, field houses, counseling centers, will know about drinking among students on this campus."

As we work in this direction, we must consider the likely result of asking people if excessive drinking does exist on campus. They will start to give opinions and attitudes and may find it hard to mention specific behavior they have observed or any data they may have accumulated. If we aren't interested in attitudes, then we focus on getting information on behavior. But if we want to investigate attitudes as well as behavior, we need another thesis: "Students, officials, and citizens are aware of campus problems caused by drinking and will have a set of attitudes toward the situation." In stating our thesis, we need to be clear about groups to query and about kinds of attitudes we expect to encounter. Anticipating reactions in this way will help us form the questions. As we specify probable attitudes, the thesis becomes more practical.

Suppose we decide to interpret this topic as referring to the problems of individual students. Instead of thinking about how excessive drinking might disturb the operation of a campus, we concern ourselves with how it might affect the drinkers themselves. The refining of the thesis might go like this:

Thesis and Hypotheses

Thesis 1:   There are students on this campus who have drinking problems.

Thesis 2:   Students who drink excessively have problems.

Thesis 3:   Students who drink excessively have problems with their school work.

These examples make no comment about cause and effect. Do academic problems cause excessive drinking, or vice-versa? Do family tensions cause drinking, or vice-versa? To establish cause and effect is difficult in any one single case, but certain facts can lead to tentative, reasonable conclusions. For example, if a student's drinking started after his or her grades started to fail, that fact, if it is a fact, would rule out the notion that drinking causes the problem.

Suppose we decide to focus this topic on the individual students who get into trouble through drinking. Let's follow the question-and-answer process through a refining of the thesis:

Question: Are there students on campus who drink excessively?

Thesis: There are students on campus who drink excessively.

Question: Do students who drink excessively get into trouble from drinking?

Thesis: Excessive drinking gets students into trouble.

Question: What kind of trouble does excessive drinking get students into?

Thesis: Students who drink excessively have problems with their academic work.

Thesis: Students who drink excessively have problems getting along with their peers.

Thesis: Students who drink excessively have problems with their families.

The thesis becomes a tool for working out your idea. Once you have sharpened your thesis, the next step is to develop testable hypotheses. These are the cutting edges necessary to carve out some information for the report. The sharper the hypothesis, the neater the information.

Thesis and Hypotheses

A *hypothesis* is a tentative proposition about a relationship between two or more phenomena, a proposition that can be empirically tested to be either true or false. These phenomena are called *variables* which must be measurable. The hypothesis must specify how the variables are related. A thesis that states "variables A and B are related" may have hypotheses such as "the greater A, the greater B," or "the more A, the less B."

Hypothesis: Excessive drinkers will have lower grade point averages than will moderate drinkers or teetotalers among the students.

Hypothesis: Excessive drinkers are more frequently dismissed from college than are moderate drinkers or teetotalers among the students.

Hypothesis: Excessive drinkers will have grade point averages that decline faster than those of moderate drinkers or non-drinkers among the students.

All of these hypotheses demand specific research. First we would have to identify the students who drink excessively. Then we would check their grades against the grades of other students and get some official records of dismissals. Some of this information may be hard to get, and even identifying "excessive drinkers" would be a problem for us to solve.

Identifying excessive drinkers is a hard job for our society in general, so we would proceed cautiously, bearing in mind that a precise definition would be unrealistic. A simple way would be to build a whole problem around the drinking habits of students. In that case, we would start with a basic question once again.

Question: What are the drinking patterns of students at this college?

Thesis: Specific drinking patterns exist at this college in quantity of alcohol consumed and consumption by sex.

Hypothesis: Male students drink more beer than female students.

Be careful not to write a hypothesis that has several different parts to it so that it might be only partially true. No clear conclusion about its accuracy will then be possible. For example: "Male students drink more beer than female students, and students drink more beer at social gatherings than they do alone." If men turn out to drink more beer than women, and students in general turn out to drink alone more often than in groups, the hypothesis is only partially true. Another possibility is that women turn out to drink the same amount of beer as do men, and that students in general drink more in social groups than alone. One way to resolve this problem is to separate the statement into two hypotheses:

1. Male students drink more beer than female students.
2. Students drink more beer socially than they do alone.

Each of these hypotheses had two variables. In the first, it is sex and amount of beer; in the second, amount of beer and degree of social involvement. Let's look at another example: Students who are very religious will drink less beer than students who are not very religious. One variable will be the degree of religiosity and the other will be the amount of beer. One more example, this time with three variables: "Students who drink excessively will have more academic problems and fewer friendships than moderate student drinkers. The variables are: amount of beer, amount of academic problems, and number of friendships.

You should form a tentative thesis and tentative hypotheses *before* your preliminary research. These tentative statements will give direction and clarity to your preliminary research. After exploring the library to see what kind of material is available, you can sharpen or completely revise your thesis and hypotheses. This can also be done after the first interview or two in the field. This two-step approach to the thesis and its hypotheses means that you make the most of your research time. The rewards of your research efforts will be greatly enhanced by the time taken to develop a clear and narrow thesis along with carefully sharpened hypotheses.

Objectivity

While forming your hypotheses, get your predispositions or value judgments into the open. Unless you are aware of these preconceptions and "suspend" them, they can bias your research and conclusions. Be honest with yourself and with your reader as you approach the topic. Here is one student explaining the context of his inquiry:

> I originally intended to examine the structure and nature of status in the high school (particularly as related to leaders) from the perspective of both high school and college students. . . . I felt that a rather fixed status structure existed in my high school, and noticed that the same students had been leaders from grammar school through high school. . . .

Though wordy, this statement clearly shows us that the writer recognizes his preconceptions might mislead as well as guide his research. To see the thesis in this statement, we simply distill the essence: "A student's collegiate status follows a pattern begun in grammar school and established by high school." In the following passage, another student frankly admits that his own experiences directly influenced his thesis:

> My anticipated results were definitely affected by my personal experiences. My devotion to my religion has floundered since I have been in college, and I have seen the same questioning and weakening of religious beliefs in several of my friends. Therefore I anticipated, on this basis only, that most students would have less religious zeal now than before college. I also assumed that this weakening. of faith would occur primarily in people with more liberal religious backgrounds, for example, Protestants and Jews, rather than Catholics. I thought that a student with a less strict religion which allowed more free thought in the first place would tend to break loose altogether when personal thought was further stimulated, as it is in college. I strongly believe that the environment in the university is indeed influential in promoting self-examination in several ways; through discussions with friends, through classes and lectures, through independence and time for thought.

Our distillation: "The collegiate environment weakens religious dedication among students, especially among members of liberal religions—Protestants and Jews." Though our concise statements may oversimplify the beliefs of these students, the compression thrusts the basic elements of their positions into sharp relief. Revealing the essentials in this way enables both writer and reader to pursue implications and applications with a sharper eye. That single sentence on religious belief lays bare the writer's essential assumption that certain religions are "more liberal" than others. Both he and his reader now need a clear idea of what he means by liberality in religion.

Making a public matter of a personal interest comes naturally, because we tend to see ourselves either in the mainstream of society or as part of an enclave either resisting or resisted by the mainstream. But be careful when your interest is more a burning conviction than an intellectual curiosity. Strong feelings tend to emphasize one aspect of a problem and bias the evidence, so make a conscious and consistent effort to take a fresh look at your subject, especially when you feel sure that research will support your favorite theory. This objectivity or "suspended judgement" is important if your readers are to trust your information and conclusions. Here is an example of a frank statement of belief, the student explaining how his personal interest translates to a public issue:

> I chose this subject for a paper because I have found myself observing the interaction of the group of students who frequent the Letters and Science Scholars' Lounge. For various reasons I found myself in the position of an accepted outsider, which I felt was ideal for close and yet relatively uninvolved observation.

He says "relatively uninvolved," and we must take his word that he has attempted to give an unbiased report. Of course the reader is predisposed to trust the writer, but the writer's candid self-assessment strengthens the report on any topic the reader may think controversial. Otherwise the reader might wonder if an objective writing style masks emotional involvement. Consider the following passage:

> My first encounter with LSD was camping last summer. I was sitting on the beach, and a friend started talking to me about a pill which could open up the other 80 percent of the human cortex. At first I was startled into disbelief, and fright followed as he impressed me as a very honest person. I had been exposed to marijuana, but he insisted that this drug had very little in common with it. He then pointed out specific people around me who had taken the drug. They were the people who were considered the oddballs, the individuals who were criticized and laughed at by adults and "normal" teenagers.

Because "encounters" with LSD can produce extremes of conviction about use of the drug, this report would be stronger with a statement of belief—especially as the writer mentions having been "exposed" to marijuana. Both because "expose" is an ambiguous word and because marijuana is another controversial topic, the writer has put himself in double jeopardy.

Your value judgements and predispositions have a dual effect. They help you discover the topic and give you insights about it. But they can also distort your work. Your closeness to the topic means, as in a friendship, special knowledge interwoven with blind spots. It is in everyone's best interest for you and your reader to be aware of those limitations.

Collecting
Data:
The Library

Chapter Four

Your hypotheses point to the kind of information necessary for testing the thesis. Now you need specific methods to collect that information. Whether you collect information primarily from the library or the field depends partly on your disposition and partly on your topic. Both kinds of research reveal the structural relations among individuals and groups, and both develop these relations by focusing on the attitudes and behavior of individuals. In field research, you gather data directly from your questions. A library paper integrates and evaluates data and opinions collected by other researchers for different purposes. Thus, in library research, you infer answers from data gathered by their research questions. Doing library research assumes two things: 1) that you can come up with a topic before entering the library—that you start with a frame with which to judge library materials, and 2) that your final thesis *will reflect your interpretation* of what has been written on the topic.

We emphasize the role of your judgment in evaluating and integrating library research to help you resist "summary fever," or "the book report syndrome," which is a danger of library research. The infected researcher loses his individuality, becoming only a recording automaton. The resulting paper, instead of weaving together information and evaluation, simply catalogs and summarizes. The cycle of whos, whats, and whens numbs the reader looking for a live mind or a point of view—an interpretation that makes the unrolling facts worth considering.

Protect yourself with the resolve to sift the readings for what applies to your thesis. Don't feel obliged to summarize each chapter or article that contains relevant material. Sources are like chunks of ore, from which you extract the elements valuable to your purpose. This refining process is an essential part of research, and it depends on your having a clear idea of your thesis. Clarity of purpose makes the processing of sources an almost automatic, yet always individual, aspect of research.

Many topics develop best from library research. Historical subjects, such as "the changing role of the American college students," or "social groupings in the American colonies," naturally take shape in the library. But studies of current phenomena are certainly possible as well. "The influence of Japanese traditions on contemporary America" or "the influence of Black Nationalists in black communities" are subjects that, when narrowed, could be examined through written sources. As these are sociological subjects, the obvious sources for their investigation would be sociological studies. Extending the search for sources along subject lines leads to checking under various headings. "Students," "college," "fraternities," "athletics," "graduate study," and "demonstrations" would be a few of the subtopics appropriate to "the changing role of the American college student."

Another tack in library work can take you to persons rather than subjects. Who might have something to say on your topic? Obviously sociologists, and thus you check sociological journals—actually forums for sociologists. That researcher of declining religious faith during college, which is a topic within the subject of the changing role of the college student, might be interested in what counselors, psychologists, psychiatrists, parents, ministers, and students have written on the topic. He or she would then check publications by and for such persons. The researcher of Black Nationalist influence could consult newspapers, books, and magazines directed specifically toward blacks or as well as writings for the white majority. This tack takes you through writing to people and again emphasizes that library research is the imaginative culling of varied sources, from sociologists to students, for the raw material necessary to test your thesis.

The Preliminary Survey

Whether most of your research is in the library or the field, you should start with a preliminary survey of the library to discover the breadth and depth of the information available on your topic. Depending on what material is available, you may shift your emphasis or, especially for a library paper, completely change the topic. This survey also limits the number of articles and books you must examine in detail. The narrowing process and the forming of tentative theses and hypotheses indicate the kind of information relevant to your work and thus sensitize you to significant titles. Our suggestions guiding you to books and articles are only a few of those possible. The point is to keep your inquiry within the scope of a term paper in sociology, to get you into the material quickly, and to prevent the stifling of your enthusiasm under a heap of references. Researchers looking for a more detailed list of sources should consult Appendix B.

Before starting to check indices, have ready several 3 × 5 index cards and your pen. When you discover a likely title, record the "locate" information on a card, which becomes a bibliography card ("bib card"). The basic "locate" information for a book would be author (or editor), title, place of publication and date. For an article, it would be author, title, source (magazine or journal), volume, date and pages. (See Appendix B for examples of these bib cards.)

You may yearn to start with the general encyclopedias, old favorites like the *Encyclopaedia Britannica*. These are almost worthless for term papers in college as they cover a world of general subjects and so have little to say on any specific topic. The bibliographies at the end of the articles may be interesting, however, and checking these will at least satisfy any need you may have to revisit these general references. Slightly more profitable is the fifteen volume *Encyclopaedia of the Social Sciences*. Keep in mind that your purpose is to see if information on your topic exists and, if it does, to what extent. So skim relevant articles and check the bibliographies following the articles. At this point you will be taking no notes, only recording the directions for finding the articles—the "locate" information.

After checking the encyclopedia sections, move to the shelves or tables of indexes. *Sources of Information in the Social Sciences: A Guide to the Literature* is a good beginning. The section "Sociology" has two parts, the first providing a concise summary of subjects in sociology and the second an annotated list of sociological sources from reviews and bibliographies to books of statistical tables and directories of unpublished information. From that guidebook you might walk a few steps to the *Social Sciences and Humanities Index* (before 1966 called the *International Index*). Depending on how much history your topic requires, check the volumes of this index under the subject headings appropriate for the topic and make a separate bib card for each article that sounds promising.

Another excellent starting point is *Sociological Abstracts*, published yearly. This source contains annotated descriptions of almost every sociological article and book published that year. Its listing is by subject, such as juvenile delinquency, collective behavior, and the family. Many journals have an annual index listing the articles for that year by title and author. Most libraries bind this index at the beginning or end of each yearly volume. In addition, two journals, *American Sociological Review* and *American Journal of Sociology,* have printed cumulative indices with updated supplements that list, by author and title, the articles published since the journals began. And both indices have a subject section similar to the one in *Sociological Abstracts*. Check the library catalog or consult a librarian to see if these sources are available. Skimming over the titles in them may give you a new angle on your topic as well as provide a list of specific references.

The goal is to assemble a satisfying number of these encouraging leads, about fifteen to fifty, for most topics, then to skim the articles and books themselves. You may need to continue this preliminary survey through other indices to assemble enough possibilities to make sure that your topic is feasible. Within reach will be the *Education Index* and the *Readers' Guide to Periodical Literature*. Nearby should be the *International Bibliography of Sociology*. We stress indices primarily listing articles because articles are by nature more specific than books and thus their application to your topic is usually clear by the title. Like a term paper, an article has a narrow scope and detailed information. A book too has detailed information, but its broader scope often makes its bearing on your topic vague. There are some efficient means to survey books, but let's set them aside for a moment.

Perhaps on seeing " 3 × 5 index cards" beginning an earlier paragraph, you remembered an unused note book lying in a desk drawer. Using it to save buying bib cards (or, later, note cards) is false economy. A notebook quickly becomes a jumble of names and numbers without the flexibility of a deck of cards. Recording the "locate" information on cards means that you can physically separate and organize them. You can put all the references to the *American Journal of Sociology* in one pile and even shuffle that pile into chronological order. Lo and behold, here are two articles in the same issue! Don't dismiss tricks like this, for they are doubly valuable: they save time, and they keep reminding you to organize the materials to your own purpose. In fact, deliberately jumbling your cards may stimulate your imagination: two titles may accidentally combine to suggest a new idea, a research lead.

Though you still shouldn't take notes on the information in the articles you check, use the bib cards to summarize their value. As you skim them, ask two questions: 1) Does it relate to my topic? and 2) How? Then simply jot brief answers on each bib card. For example, the student wondering about the decline in students' religious faith might have this note: "Sociologist finds religious background of college students (at Northwestern) important in attitudes toward sex. Good questions about strength of belief. Recheck." Another card might show: "Compares attitudes toward lay teachers and priests in Catholic schools. Might fit." Another might simply record: "No good." Skimming the sources and marking the value of each source enables you to sift material rapidly. The preliminary survey ends when you think you've seen the extent of your topic and can fairly select the most relevant information. An afternoon spent combing indices and skimming articles gives you a solid base for thorough research as well as the satisfaction of getting yourself started.

Data: The Library

Your preliminary survey might include a check of the card catalog for relevant books. But don't spend more than an hour there, because books really are comprehensive sources. Becoming familiar with the focused topics of articles helps you select from the broader coverage of books. In the same way the bibliographies accompanying articles will be more specific than those included in books. If one of the articles has mentioned a promising book, jot its author and title on a bib card and check the card catalog under the author's name. Checking there instead of under the title might lead you to another of the same author's books on the same subject. If the card catalog indexes the book, note its call number on the bib card. Don't rush to look it up if you have access to the stacks; keep probing the card catalog. *If the stacks are closed to you, order the book immediately.* Otherwise delays in an overtaxed college library can hamstring you.

Next check the card catalog under the subject headings related to the topic, noting the call number, the author's name and the title of the book. Again, by using cards instead of a notebook, you can organize the likely books according to call number; if you have stack access this organization saves your having to run from one side of the library to the other (and perhaps from floor to floor in a large library). Without stack access you have no choice but to order the most likely sounding titles. On receiving them, check the tables of contents and then the indices to see if any section is relevant. With your narrow topic it is extremely unlikely that the whole book will apply. Thus you can quickly determine the books requiring more careful examination. Keep them and return the rest—another student may need them.

If you can enter the stacks, head for the section corresponding to the call numbers of most of your possible titles and start sifting again. Running an eye across the shelved books, check the whole section for titles that you may have overlooked in the card catalog. In this way an amazing amount of work can be done in a couple of hours at the card catalog and in the stacks. Selecting books with pertinent information and rejecting others is far more invigorating than hauling a pile of books away with the intention of skimming them later. For many students such a pile becomes a monument to good intentions—a heap of tomes difficult to open and inaccessible to other researchers. Researching library materials in the library keeps the work more efficient and less burdensome than if it has to compete with the distractions of home.

Beyond the general indices and the card catalog lie a vast number of other possible references. *Sources of Information in the Social Sciences* lists those in sociology and closely related disciplines. If you need more, check with the reference librarian, a live source usually delighted to use his or her extensive knowledge of library materials—especially if you have already done some spadework. Remember that it doesn't take long to check the relevance of sources if your topic is narrow. Two or three afternoons of preliminary skimming can develop enough sources for nearly every library paper. Of course, taking notes on the significant articles and books requires more time.

Taking Notes

The bib cards record only essential "locate" information plus a comment or two about their potential for your topic. "Note cards" (4 × 6 is a good size) record the pertinent information from the articles and books. When you feel confident that your sifting has revealed enough titles to produce a paper, settle down to careful reading and thoughtful notetaking. Consider each author's purpose, method, findings, and conclusions, and take notes on information bearing on your hypotheses or thesis. Remember that *your purpose is not to summarize the article or book for your reader, but to use it fairly to develop your own point.*

A note should nearly always refer to a specific page and have the page number clearly noted on the card. A reference to "pp. 12-17" is too general. Because notecards record specifics related to your topic, each 4 × 6 card should record only one item of information—a fact or an opinion, an assumption or a conclusion, a single quotation or a paraphrase. If by some chance a note runs beyond one side of a card, put it on a second card instead of on the back of the original card. One card means no more than one item. For example, the following statement contains two items of information: "One-fourth of the students were Catholic, and one-third of these belonged to fraternities." The original writer's study linked these items, but our student diligently working on declining faith in college would probably use only one of them. If both were relevant, they might fit in separate sections of the paper. Using one card per item means you can eventually organize piles of notecards to correspond with the divisions of an outline. Be sure to distinguish your own words from those of the source, perhaps using, in addition to quotation marks, a different ink or a wavy marginal line. (For more specific suggestions and examples, see Appendix B.)

Reread your notecards after finishing an article; forgotten page numbers or mistakes in wording are easy to correct with the article at hand. Nothing is more frustrating than discovering such an error later, rerequesting the book or article, finding it charged out to another researcher, and having to guess. Also check the corresponding bib card to make sure it includes the information necessary for the final bibliography. Plan to get your information at one sitting. Don't think that if you possess the book and take it home, you possess its information. Even a photocopy can mislead you into thinking that you've done something significant with the source. When you sit down to organize your information, it should be complete in your stack of notecards, easy to shuffle, sort, arrange, rearrange, and reject as your organization dictates. A stack of notecards is more manageable and casts a much lighter shadow than a stack of books.

Our goal is to give you a framework for notetaking and make some suggestions; the quality of the notes depends upon your vision. The best guides to notetaking, for the term paper as a whole, are a definite interest in your topic and a clear preliminary thesis.

Collecting
Data:
The Field

Chapter Five

A "field research project" may sound intimidating, but if properly restricted it is quite manageable—even enjoyable. Preliminary work gives you a context for the field work, with most of your time in a field project going toward organizing, collecting, and analyzing questionnaires, interviews, observations.

In a field research project you are practically immune to the book report syndrome. Being involved in collecting evidence on your own or with a team of students makes writing a lifeless report nearly impossible. But even a dull report on a field project, one that only told the story of the field work and used unanalyzed data as its substance, would clearly rest on original effort. As one student pointed out, field research vividly demonstrates the obstacles and rewards of sociology:

> So the sociologist is an intricate blend of skilled perceptive, experienced, creative qualities as well as an intelligent and patient worker. Enter the . . . student with the role of playing The Sociologist and with the expectation of a rather detailed written analysis of his Project to be subjected to the scrutiny of The Sociology Professor. This paper, then, is more the story of how the student failed in playing The Sociologist, but, in failing, learned finally what a sociologist is supposed to do and developed an appreciation of the arts and skills the sociologist must possess.

The first step in field research is to describe the sociological issue to be examined. Chapter Three, which explained this step as the development of the thesis and relevant hypotheses, is worth a brief review. Consider this explanation of one student's thesis:

> The relationship between an artist and his public has always been an illusive one. The viewer is definitely a vital interest in an artist's life but whether or not this influence is felt during the process of creation is difficult to analyze. Even if this element is established as having direct effect, the degree of this influence is even more vague. Art, being an ultimately emotional response, is easy to accept *per se* because of its illusiveness. One tends to do very little reasoning about the values and motives which act beneath the surface. In this field, there seems to be an aura of intangibility concerning the relationship between the artist, the work of art, and the viewer. This study takes a look at a small group of artists and their beliefs concerning the creative process.

The hypotheses would point to specific evidence supporting the thesis. "Evidence" would be statements by artists and the researcher's observations of the artists and their work. Without hypotheses, the investigation—the interviewing—would be random and the results vague. What does the researcher expect to discover? "Creative artists will be unable to explain coherently what influence the public has on their work. Their statements and answers will be inconsistent, muddled and in contradiction to such observable influences as suggestions from instructors and patrons." Good hypotheses will alert you to data that supports the thesis, but be ready to recognize evidence to the contrary. In fact, a good exercise to assure the actual testing of your hypotheses is to create contrary assumptions. These re-statements need not be brand new ideas, just the reversal of your hypotheses. An example of a contrary hypothesis appropriate to this study of artists would be: "Creative artists will clearly, consistently and realistically point out the outside influences on their work." A little contrariness keeps your eyes and ears open for all the relevant evidence.

Selecting a Group

Information in the field always comes ultimately from individuals, but the sociological perspective interprets this information to show the individual's role in a group. The student observing artists developed the thesis from the experience of being one of a group of artists. Selecting a group you know or are a part of is convenient, but base your study on more than convenience. The artist formed a thesis on an idea that came from casual observation. The term paper was an opportunity to test that idea. Another student's project developed from experience selling doughnuts. Casual observation of customers indicated that college women were quick to exploit an honor system of payment. The student saw both theoretical and practical implications in the study, since the group was the clientele, as this comment frankly explains:

> In this study the honor system constituted the basis for a doughnut service delivering doughnuts five mornings a week, Monday through Friday, to various Isla Vista and Goleta locations of college students and working non-students. Due to lack of time in the mornings (delivery could not begin before seven o'clock at most places, and the writer had a nine o'clock class every morning) and the difficulty of finding feasible consumer markets (residence halls were too large to be adequately serviced and individual apartments produced too little demand), it was impossible to include many social sub-groups of students. Thus, seven sorority houses had to serve as a college student sample. (No fraternities expressed any interest in the service.) The working, non-students were comprised of employees of the state and county governments and small, independent businesses.

The thesis was straightforward: "College women will react to an honor system differently than will the full-time employees along the route."

Data: The Field

The way both the artist and the doughnut deliverer worked to a thesis from direct experience with a group might be considered inductive—reasoning from the specifics of experience with a group to the general ideas of thesis and topic. In an earlier example we deduced our group by reasoning from the topic of medical abortion to "thirty obstetricians practicing in Siesta City, California." The inductive and deductive methods of choosing a group are equally good. Pick the one that suits your interest.

Restricting a group to a few persons enables you to study them in detail if the opportunity to question and observe is unlimited. But a questionnaire sent to ten people provides less information than the same questionnaire sent to a hundred. By choosing a group small enough so that you can contact each member, you can draw conclusions that apply to *that* group as a whole. But extending those conclusions beyond the group raises a problem. If you were to study "present U.S. Senators," your conclusions might fit the whole group (provided you heard from everyone), and your audience would be interested because this group influences people all over the world. But how important are conclusions about the campus ski club? This is not to say that such a study would be sociologically mistaken, only that its findings would have restricted application. The desire of most researchers to make findings widely applicable causes them to select a relatively small group (or sample) which represents a much larger group. We saw how the doughnut seller selected a group by the limits of the sales route. But instead of concluding that some women in those two sorority houses were dishonest, the researcher wants to extend findings about the dishonesty of these few women to "college students." Similarly, the artist-researcher assumes that the group studied is a sample of artists and thus the findings will apply to artists in general. The validity of generalizing from sample to population depends on the characteristics of the population and the procedures for selecting the representative group.

Sampling

Choosing an ideal sample from populations like "doctors" or "college students" takes an expert. But as your project is a term paper and not a textbook, we will discuss only a selected few of the considerations appropriate to making a good sample. Number one: *don't sacrifice fairness to convenience.* Investigating a thesis about "students in sociology'' by passing out a questionnaire to a dozen friends in your class is only a step above filling out a dozen yourself. Fight such corruption. The ridiculous example of unfairness is the Martian who lands in a field of cows and thinks he-she-it is sampling the opinions of Earthlings. Had the researcher made a preliminary survey, it might at least have included a few cockroaches. This kind of thoughtless, arbitrary sampling is the kind popularly—and mistakenly—considered "random." It is done for the researcher's convenience and assumes that anyone who satisfies one population requirement (American, student, doctor) is likely to represent accurately the characteristics of that population.

In the sociologist's random sample, every person in the group under study has an equal chance of being questioned. In this way, "systematic bias" in sample selection is minimized and chances increase of getting a sample that accurately represents the total group. Ideally, you would put the names of everyone in the group in a hat or computer, shake well, and pull out your sample. But usually you can't get a complete list of names and must use less careful methods. Consider first the reason for your study and list the characteristics that might be important, then identify where persons with those characteristics can be found. For example, if you are interested in attitudes of New Yorkers toward the police, interviewing only on Park Avenue would no doubt underrepresent blacks, Puerto Ricans and almost everyone else except the well-to-do. But note: One reason such a "sample" is inadequate is that the topic is unrealistic.

For a perhaps more familiar example, consider the influence of living away from home on the diets of college students. Before you select a sample, pass out your questionnaires, and start to interview, reflect on what you know of the population. Common sense suggests that the campus "homes" of students would have a bearing on the results. Students living in dormitories, fraternity and sorority houses, apartments, with relatives, alone, in twos and threes, in large groups, and in mated pairs might all have different eating patterns. A dinner prepared by a sorority house dietician might be worlds apart from one assembled in a commune. Passing out your questionnaires only in dormitories would be likely to bias your sample, and the bias would also appear if you passed them out only in supermarkets near campus.

One approach to the problem would be to gather facts on the proportion of the students falling into various housing patterns; the other is to modify the topic. An alternative thesis would follow:

Data: The Field

"Living in dormitories influences the diets of students." Even then you might consider the interesting possibilities of sampling for that topic. Suppose dormitory residents come from all economic levels. Very likely the diets of the poor students would improve, and perhaps the diets of the rich would suffer. Based on this common-sense reasoning, the sampling would require a knowledge of the proportion of students in various economic categories. You can see that choosing a thesis and selecting a sample are interrelated decisions. Again, the limited time available for a term paper prevents you from skirting all the pitfalls the professional sociologists so carefully try to avoid. They expect to err, and so should you. But follow in their footsteps as far as you can in being fair, thoughtful, and thorough.

The Questionnaire

Preparing, distributing, and analyzing a scientifically reliable questionnaire also requires knowledge beyond the scope of the term paper. But just as in selecting a sample, the complexities need not deter you from doing your best and then learning from the effort. The point is to discover what a questionnaire involves—what makes it successful and what creates problems. Developing a completely unbiased questionnaire and administering it well require more time and money than a student can afford. But you can compensate somewhat for these limitations by carefully considering the kind of information most useful for your thesis and the nature of the group to be surveyed.

A questionnaire is generally a form the respondent fills out without any help or comment from the researcher. It enables data to be collected from large samples, but it requires careful construction because it depends solely on the respondent's perception of the questions and his or her good will in taking the time to complete it. Whether you distribute a questionnaire or conduct interviews, you must make every effort to be sure the questions are in good form. That means each question must be easily understood by your respondents and must elicit the specific information needed to test the hypotheses. To ask a respondent a question irrelevant to your hypotheses wastes both the respondent's time and yours. When you have checked the questions for their clarity and relevance, the next step is to check their effectiveness. One way is to *pretest* the questionnaire. Select six to ten people who have similar characteristics to those in your sample and have them fill out the questionnaire. The pretest should include the opportunity for the respondents to comment, either in conversation or in notes, on the clarity of each question and the appropriateness of the answers. This allows you to revise doubtful questions before distributing it to your sample. The researcher should also examine these pre-test responses to see if the data are in the form needed for testing the hypotheses. Nothing is more frustrating than to find out after all the data are collected that you should have asked an additional or more specific question.

The pretest has two important don'ts: 1) *Don't* ask any person whom you intend to be part of the sample to pretest your questionnaire or interview schedule. If this happens inadvertently, *don't* include that data in your analysis of the sample. 2) *Don't* attempt to analyze the pretest data to test or revise your hypotheses. It will be tempting to do so, but analysis is bound to lead you towards false conclusions. The value of the pretest is as a test for your questions, not your hypotheses. Use it, but don't abuse it.

Unless you personally distribute and pick it up or can use a free campus mail, the questionnaire requires enough money to cover postage for four mailings: the original mailing, including a stamped return envelope, and a follow-up mailing, also including a stamped return. (If you are optimistic, the follow-up may simply be a reminder that assumes the respondent still can locate the questionnaire and its return envelope.) Distributing the material in person has the added value of personal contact, which might boost the percentage of returns. Otherwise be prepared for disappointment because mail questionnaires commonly have a low percentage of response.

Don't ignore the attitudes of non-respondents as they may be important. A survey of professors that asks, "What kinds of projects do you believe are best for students?" might be spurned by opponents of original research by undergraduates. Generalizations about "professors" on the data from a fifty percent return would be biased. This character of the non-respondents remains unsettlingly mysterious unless a phone call, visit, or letter can clarify their reluctance. Most often non-respondents simply haven't gotten around to acting on their good intentions. Keep their numbers few by means of polite reminders. Telephone calls to delinquent respondents are usually effective. Some researchers have gone so far as to include an attractive pencil or shiny coin with the first request as an incentive, but a tactful letter is usually as successful and better suited to your altruistic project.

George Gallup, Sr., the famous pollster, has suggested five types of questions for data collection. Each type elicits a different type of information.

Filter or Information Question—If you plan to ask people their opinions about a topic, you must determine how much information or thought each subject has given to the issue. People often are willing to give their opinions about anything, whether they are familiar with it or not, so if you want people with knowledge, ask a question to filter out those ignorant of the topic. A straightforward "Have you heard or read anything about X situation?" is a filter question. If you think that the respondents' prior knowledge of the subject may significantly influence the results, you may find it valuable to briefly test the extent of their knowledge. Asking for the "pros" and "cons" of an issue, or for the basic components of Proposition B, would help you assess this prior knowledge. Be careful not to intimidate respondents, especially if they seem to have little or no knowledge about the issue. If you find that about half your subjects have at least some knowledge of the issue and the other half have little or no knowledge, you might test the hypotheses separately for each group.

Open or Free Question—This type allows the respondents to answer in their own words, and it can produce strikingly original information. But it also may result in vague, rambling remarks that are impossible to tabulate and analyze, so use this type of question selectively. Examples of open questions are: What do you think of having Federal gun control legislation? What effect will be unemployment rate have upon your vote in future national elections?

Structured or Specific Question—This type provides a definite set of answers to choose from. The structured question is harder to construct as the possible choices must be figured out and then arranged to prevent bias, but the answers (yes-no or multiple choice) are easy to tabulate and analyze, especially if transferred to IBM cards. The danger in simplifying the choices for ease of analysis is the possibility of oversimplifying the issue. "Would you cheat on an exam?" is a crucial question in establishing information about the honesty of students, but it may be so bold that respondents who would cheat hesitate to mark their true answer. They might object, "What about the circumstances? Those are important for me." Sometimes, however, simplification can force respondents to reveal a true position that multiple choice or open-ended questions might obscure. "Would you cheat on an exam if you knew that most of the class were cheating?" Providing only yes-no alternatives for that question might force true answers by clearly presenting an ethical extreme. On the other hand, making it open-ended might reveal an interesting range of values: "If I needed a passing grade in that course to stay in school, yes." Perhaps wording the question a little differently might take even better advantage of the open-ended freedom to respond: "Under what circumstances would you cheat on an exam?" That's a deliberately loaded question allowing respondents to answer, "Under no circumstances," but it suggests that they analyze their own experience and ethics. Then they might answer, "Only if I felt sure of getting away with it." There are other considerations in choosing the type of questions, as the following comments by a student-researcher testify:

> In making up the questionnaire, questions with a "yes" or "no" were used in hopes of insuring a higher response, for it was felt that questions that required writing would tend to inhibit people and thereby reduce the number that would return the survey. Also, "inbetween" type answers such as "maybe" or "I don't know" were avoided for fear people would shy away from the issues and seek refuge in such an answer. This and other factors in the questionnaire lead [sic] to several problems which will be discussed later. Comments were asked for and a relatively large number did make remarks which were quite helpful, both in expanding their stated views and in pointing out flaws in the questionnaire.

Reason Why Question— This can be an effective probe when subjects have been asked to state an opinion on a specific issue. It may be combined with an open question: What do you think about the teachers' strike? Briefly, why do you feel this way? Or it may follow a structured question: Do you plan to go on for graduate studies? (Yes. No. Why?)

Intensity Question—This last type is to determine how strongly a respondent may feel about an opinion or response. Though a majority of respondents may agree with a certain issue, their intensity of agreement may vary greatly. This type of question often fits the structured form: What do you think of our current foreign policy? (Strongly agree, Moderately agree, Moderately disagree, Strongly disagree.) It

Data: The Field

may be wise to avoid a neutral response category, for respondents may choose what they consider safe middle ground rather than take time to evaluate their true feelings.

The liberal range of possible questions enables you to construct those best for your purpose. (See Appendix C.) In working up your questions, experiment with different wordings to sharpen the points you want to test and to make them clear, concise, and answerable. Keep in mind the experience and attitudes of your audience. They may interpret your words far differently than you intend, so pretest the questionnaire. At least have a friend take it and comment, but try to pretest it with a few people from the total group but not from your sample. Their reactions will give you a chance to reword ambiguous questions and discard unprofitable ones before committing your time and expense to the actual survey. Be especially wary of vague questions or those that produce only "acceptable" or "natural" answers, as one student found common in his survey:

> Why do these two-thirds come to the lounge? What do they do when there? These were two other questions posed on the questionnaires. The answers to these questions overlapped to such an extent that they might as well have been combined. One finds a great similarity between the answers given by the thirty-five respondents, for they all run in the same vein. The typical answers went: goof off, play bridge, sit and talk, listen to music, enjoy the atmosphere, relax, meet people, and a very representative answer—"I just come to see if anything is going on."

Discovering flaws in his questionnaire probably taught this student more about sociological inquiry than any suggestions we could include in this manual—or that he might hear in weeks of lectures.

A little more thought about what he expected might have led to better questions, but then every researcher finds weaknesses in his questionnaire. And sometimes only actual results reveal a defect. The student would have done better by specifying choices if he suspected that lounge activities like bridge and listening to music were means to some other end.

1. Which one of these activities do you intend most often to join when coming to the lounge?
   a. playing bridge   b. listening to music   c. studying   d. resting
   e. talking   f. other (specify) _____

2. What are you primarily seeking in joining that lounge activity?
   a. relaxation   b. stimulation   c. friendship   d. company
   e. distraction   f. other (specify) _____

(Leaving a little space after a structured question often leads to interesting information.) Keep in mind that questions developing facts and attitudes should be as specific as possible. In the above example, two students could now record the same factual answer to the first question (e.g., a. playing bridge) but different answers to the second (e.g., b. stimulation; f. money—we play a penny a point), a complexity overlooked in the original survey.

A student attempting to discover professors' perceptions of college asked this open-ended question: "What are the disadvantages of large classes?" Note that the wording points the response toward two considerations—large classes and disadvantages. An alternative wording could reverse directions and add an idea: "What advantages do large classes offer the student? The instructor?" The original question's mirror image, "What are the advantages of small classes?" should develop essentially the same information as the original. These questions also suggest a prior consideration: "What do you consider a large class?" The researcher could provide some choices or leave it open-ended to see what developed. There could be another prior question: "What advantages and disadvantages of class size depend on the type of class?"

But isn't there some limit to these questions within questions?

Yes. You must decide which questions are essential because you and your respondent are only human. He or she can't take the time to consider pages and pages of questions whose purpose is not clear. And you yourself have to get somewhere before the term ends. In the mail questionnaire for a term paper, the respondent should not be asked to give more than ten or fifteen minutes. Pretest your questionnaire to make certain that most respondents can answer in this amount of time without rushing—but if you pretest on friends, remember that they may respond especially rapidly and eagerly (depending on your friends, of course).

Factual questions such as age, sex and marital status are easy to answer and thus are good starters for the questionnaire. If possible, salt other factual queries throughout to relieve the respondent's struggle with questions of opinion or interpretation. Keep the questionnaire suited to your purpose in choice, wording and placement of questions, but at the same time make it appealing to the respondent. And if you have questions that might shock or embarrass some persons, put those near the end and then leave a space labeled "additional comments." That will allow an irate respondent to blow off steam, instead of tossing the questionnaire in the trashcan.

The Interview

Interviews impose on the respondent even more than mail questionnaires, but most persons cooperate in interviews, especially if they sympathize with the interviewer. Perhaps the opportunity for personal contact redeems the extra time and interruption. Just as you would introduce a mail questionnaire with a letter, begin your encounter with the respondent by tactfully asking for the person's help and acknowledging the demand on his or her time. Without apology, briefly explain that the information is necessary for your term paper in sociology; but avoid explaining your thesis or hypotheses, as that might bias the respondent. Say who you are, where you're from, and what you're doing. "I'm Joan Smith from Thompson College, and I'm doing some work for a term paper project in sociology." Then ask for cooperation and briefly explain the project. "I would appreciate it if you could take a few minutes to help me get a little information on the lifestyles of this area." Get to your questions as quickly as possible, moving from factual ones to those touching attitudes, leaving the sensitive questions until near the end. Saving two or three routine questions for the end, however, may relieve any awkwardness or tension that might develop. The interview can be maddening, but it can also be rewarding for the same reason: it embodies the spontaneity of a human relationship.

A good open-end interview clarifies your thesis, but a responsive subject doesn't always mean a good interview. Profit by the sad experience of another student:

> I compiled so much varied and unrelated information through these interviews that many papers could have been developed from this survey emphasizing one or another of the many aspects involved. This was perhaps due to the nature of the open-end interview, but certainly due also to the fact that I neglected to direct or restrict their answers to any great extent.

Before starting your interview, then, do some hard thinking about the best questions to ask in order to test your hypotheses. And think about the attitudes you are likely to encounter, and about how the respondent will react to your requests and queries. It is important to develop and pretest the interview schedule before collecting the data. Do not assume you will develop or improve the form of the questions as you go along. If you do not ask each respondent the same questions in the same form and sequence, tabulating and summarizing the data will be difficult. You might even seriously bias or distort the quality of the data.

Quite likely, the ticklish possibilities will suggest that you develop a structured schedule of questions to guide the interview. This "interview schedule" may actually be a questionnaire that will be given verbally. But it can be this, and more. Personal interviewing allows you to probe for answers on delicate questions or with hesitant respondents. The probing may be no more than asking for clarification or elaboration, but it may also be a way of penetrating beneath surface appearances or glib reactions.

With key questions, it is best to prepare some of these probes (a little more hard thinking before you begin). In the following example, explicit questions are followed by open-ended probes:

[1] a. Are you ever depressed about things in your life?
    b. How frequently, would you say?
    c. About what sort of things usually?
    d. What do you find is a good thing to do when you feel that way?

[2] Over the last ten or fifteen years, do you feel that your family has been doing better_____, about the same_____, or not doing so well_____?
    Why? (In what way?) _____

Not all probing need be planned, however. In fact, a perceptive interviewer can sometimes make discoveries through a respondent's chance remark or vocal inflection. Though you will have a pattern in mind for the interview, be sensitive to the respondent's hesitations, inflections, facial movements, and gestures—they tell a story. Of course, well worded questions and a polite, warm, straightforward manner will develop most of your information. The exploration should be done within a planned framework, but for most topics the best interviews partake of conversational depth, involving both you and the respondents without biasing their attitudes or clouding your judgment.

> At first, it was thought that a questionnaire would be more efficient; but as it proved, interviewing was much more effective. The idea of talking to a woman of their own age about these things put them at ease, and through extraneous conversation, much valuable information was obtained.

For some highly touchy subjects (but fewer than you might expect) or in cases where your subject demands that the interview be warm and open, notes may be inhibiting. One approach to this is to use a small portable tape recorder. You will be surprised at how few respondents will refuse or even bridle at its use. Some even open up in its presence. *Do not* secretly tape an interview. Hoodwinking your respondent is unethical. It could also be illegal. Before you begin the interview, *ask the respondent's permission* to tape the session for efficiency and accuracy. Reassure him or her that you will not let anyone else hear the tape and that you will erase it when the project is completed. Then be very sure you keep these promises. The interview is a matter of trust between the respondent and you. Never violate that trust.

If it is not possible to use a tape recorder or to take detailed notes, take crucial notes during the interview. Immediately after the interview, transfer them to your interview schedule. Then take a few more minutes to analyze what happened, with an eye to improving subsequent interviews. Here is one student's experience:

> The first appointments were with familiar teachers; these prepared me for teachers who were strangers. Because of the nature of the project, I wanted to make the interviews as relaxed and casual as possible; thus, I used no papers and took no notes on what the person said. This proved to be a mistake because the results cannot be more specific than generalizations. After the first six interviews I formulated a type of schedule which I used to direct the interview and the remaining interviews were more organized. With several teachers I tried to take notes but this was disconcerting and the answers were much freer when the teacher didn't feel he or she was being quoted on every off-color remark.

Construct your interview schedule along the lines suggested in our preceding section; then try it out by pretesting it with "trial" members of the group being studied. Your experience and their suggestions will smooth your technique and improve the questions. Note especially how your own verbal and visual inflections change your information. Stressing different words in the same question provokes different answers. Contrast "Would you *feel* like cheating in those circumstances?" with "Would *you* feel like cheating in those circumstances?" Your looks may also influence the respondents, but changing your clothes or hair to "pass" as a member of a widely different group is difficult because social milieux are complex patterns of dress, speech and actions. One student describes her reception in a San Francisco locale:

> The group seemed to sense immediately that I was not one of them, and they seemed hostile toward me as a result. In retrospect, it is very difficult to pinpoint the direct cause of my terror, so perhaps it was merely a combination of circumstances and conditions which shocked me. Several times women hissed and screamed in my face, while others were abnormally affectionate. It was impossible for me to accustom myself to the lurking oddities, yet I tried to remain calm and objective.

If your respondents are part of your daily life (teachers, neighbors, fellow students), see if their behavior matches their answers.

> I also noticed, in observing students, that nearly all were very receptive to the instructor's criticism, and they were often followed through with his suggestions, even though the artist basically disagreed. Even among those students who had been so strong in their convictions about artists creating for themselves, there were many who noticeably changed their work to please an instructor.

How does the writer know these artists changed their work to please an instructor? The researcher might have asked directly, "Are you making that change to please the instructor?" Such a direct question might hit a tender nerve and be painful for both interviewer and respondent. But a more tactful approach might draw a sheepish admission from the artist that his or her ethics were a bit more complicated than the artist realized or was willing to admit:

I. "Seems to me you're trying something a little different in that painting. Get a new idea?"

R. "Well, actually that's the instructor's idea. He thinks I need a 'unifying element'."

Data: The Field

Don't attempt to trick your respondents by posing as someone other than a student gathering information for a term paper. As Kai T. Erikson suggests, two ethical principles in social research should be carefully noted: "First, that it is unethical for a sociologist to *deliberately misrepresent* his [or her] identity for the purpose of entering a private domain *to which he [or she] is not otherwise eligible*; and second, that it is unethical for a sociologist to *deliberately misrepresent* the character of the research in which he [or she] is engaged."*

Allen Barton's article "Asking the Embarrassing Question," cited at the end of Appendix C, cleverly suggests some effective ways to ask the question you anticipate will touch a sensitive area. One final note: the coding method should be set up even before you pretest the questionnaire. Then you can pretest both the questions and the coding to see that you have the information in the form needed to test the hypotheses.

Don't crowd your questions on the sheet even if you record the answers yourself. The page will quickly become confusion, costing time and increasing errors. For open-ended questions, leave more space than you think you need, and keep spare paper handy. The major advantage of questions involving a limited range of response ("yes" or "no"; "Democrat" or "Republican"; "a great deal," "somewhat," or "very little") is that they can be readily converted into tables. But the advantage quickly becomes burdensome if you fail to plan for it. Arrange the spaces for responses to such questions *vertically*, and place them at the left edge of the paper; that allows you to set up a tabulation sheet that can be used easily and accurately (see Appendix E). Such planning takes time, but the time returns.

Observation of Behavior

We all know the "researcher" who goes to bars, cocktail parties, and topless shows "to observe the people." And we all fool ourselves some of the time in confusing our experiences and "the facts." A few vague observations and a little hearsay sweep us to generalizations

*"A Comment on Disguised Observation in Sociology," *Research Methods: Issues and Insights*, eds. Billy J. Franklin and Harold W. Osborne (Belmont, Calif.: Wadsworth Publishing Company, Inc., 1971), p. 74.

about "today's youth" or "people over thirty." But sociology assumes considered and careful observation, so you should reexamine familiar situations with new eyes. The resulting perceptions will stimulate both you and your reader.

Suppose that during an ordinary experience like attending a hockey game you set out to discover something simple based on some details of behavior. Details usually disregarded will now leap out at you. The fans first seem perfect examples of categories—stereotypes. Couples on dates, businessmen bussed in by a local tavern, dyed-in-the-wool rooters leaning over the boards, players on the bench and in the penalty boxes, screaming high school groups, sober and loyal graduate students, husbands and wives out for an evening, solitary middle-aged men, pairs of middle-aged women, the drunks, the drugged, the restless addicts of the snack bar.

As you look closer, details suggest subtler classifications than "hockey fan." In a few seconds you locate the "Monday-morning quarterback"—a fan who knows what should have been done and who believes in letting others share his hindsights. After a few minutes of observation, you can see several types of these after-the-fact analysts. Two seats away is a curly-haired woman who places her open right hand against a corner of her mouth and shouts, using her hand as a half-megaphone. The man two rows down and half a dozen seats to the left uses both of his hands cupped together to amplify and focus his shouts. Another, in the second row, at the two goals scored against the home team, turns to the fans sitting above him and implores, "Go home! Go home! These guys get nervous with people watching. We should all go home and watch TV. The basketball game." One has a player's number: "Eighty-six! Eighty-six! Ya let him get by! Give 'em some body English. Get tough." After each shout she notes something on her program, as if keeping score on eighty-six. A man behind and to the right sits hunched in a parka, hands in his pockets. Each error he sees draws him forward to shout between the couple in front of him, "Seven below outside. Might as well stay."

As you accumulate these observations, form some new categories. What subgroups can you pick out of the general group called "Monday-morning quarterbacks"? Shouters, for one. How could you further classify? Maybe by noting the supposed audience of each shouter: the players, the coach, a companion, the crowd in general. By noting characteristics such as sex, age, body type, you could classify these groups as "homogeneous," sharing many characteristics, or

Data: The Field

"heterogeneous," sharing few. If the shouters had all been male, about the same age, and dressed similarly, the group would have been homogeneous. As our example stands, however, the group is heterogeneous.

The ideal term paper in sociology would draw its data from observations, interviews, questionnaires, books, articles, statistical and historical records. But no one looks for the ideal. Your reader expects only sincere and systematic efforts to discover something for yourself about people and about the analysis of groups. The more time you allow yourself, the more thoughtful will be your approaches and the more likely will be your satisfaction with your work. If you wait until the last minute to discover the facts, they will overwhelm you in a rush. Do what is reasonable and possible. Be encouraged by the knowledge that every writer, including your instructor must cope with limitations.

Analyzing
the
Information

Chapter Six

"In the final analysis"—at last that cliché comes alive as you compare the results of your study with the predictions of your hypotheses. For this will be the final rather than the first analysis of your accumulating data. If you pretested your questionnaire or your interview technique, the purpose of the pretest was to analyze for biased or inconclusive data and allow you to improve the method. Your library research may have uncovered more than one set of facts or opinions on your topic, which require you to analyze the source of the difference and to seek further support for one of the sets. You may also have been able to compare the results of your survey with the findings of another researcher using a similar survey or studying a similar group. Such intermediate analysis develops as naturally as one book leads to another in systematic research, and it makes the final analysis an extension of a process rather than the start of a problem.

The final analysis begins when the information that tests your hypotheses lies before you in piles of note cards and questionnaires. Like most researchers, you may still feel that another batch of questionnaires should be sent out to clarify a foggy point or correct a glaring mistake from your first batch. It may seem that one more fact will plug a yawning gap in your argument. Despite these feelings, you must suspend research and start writing in time to meet your instructor's deadline and finish your other courses. If you have worked conscientiously in the library or have collected as many questionnaires as your reminders can produce or have interviewed everyone in your sample, set your doubts aside and begin evaluating the information in hand. Your thesis and corresponding hypotheses have given you a pretty good idea of what those piles of note cards or questionnaires contain. You don't ask "What does it all mean?"—at least, not at first. The question is "Does it confirm or contradict my hypotheses?"

At this point pride may tempt you to force the data to support your thesis. Twisting the information to prove yourself right would completely betray your data and the purpose of research. As we said earlier, negative conclusions can be valuable. They lead you and your reader to examine skeptically a conventional "truth" about part of society, a truth that may have otherwise seemed "obvious," even to you. Research tests belief as well as discovering the unthought. The life in one student's report stemmed from his reaction to negative data.

> When considering how to approach the topic of characteristics common to lounge-users, I turned to a paper I had written about six weeks previously on that subject. To my surprise, *nothing* I had stated in that paper was any longer valid. Something had changed—was it the scholars or was it me?

He could have been embarrassed that his previous findings were mistaken, but the discovery stimulated his curiosity. The curious researcher then overcame the embarrassed student.

Neutral or negative findings require that you either revise your thesis or assume your study was either inadequate or faulty. Perhaps your original thesis is valid, but more research would be necessary to outweigh the negative findings. On the other hand, remember that your original thesis was tentative—a device to focus your research. If you have no evidence that the data are wrong, then they *are* the reality your research set out to describe. If this reality is false, it will take the data from another research project to discover the mistake.

Comparing, and perhaps contrasting, the tentative thesis and corresponding hypotheses with your findings is the normal procedure of a research project, and revising the thesis is permissible. But in writing your report, don't conceal the fact that your beginning assumptions led to hypotheses that research disproved. In other words, don't alter history to make yourself look good. Sometimes the new findings are more welcome than the predicted ones. Suppose a researcher begins a market survey of college students assuming that they buy primarily books, records, clothing, movie tickets, and gasoline. Then the survey shows that the students in the sample spent hundreds of dollars each on trips, sports equipment, phonographs, and guitars. Either the study is biased (bad sample or poor questionnaire) or the thesis is askew. Plenty of maufacturers and retailers would eagerly vote for revising the thesis, though they might like to see a confirming study before investing in new advertising campaigns.

Analyzing Library Research

Evaluating your notes on the work of other researchers means classifying the information according to aspects of your hypotheses. For example, if you began by assuming that the first experience with heroin for many addicts came during military service, one category would be "military" and another "first experience." One category organizes all your information on drug use by servicemen; the second embraces all the data on the first taste of heroin. Even though your research failed to turn up significant figures to prove the hypothesis, it might suggest something just as valuable about either addicted servicemen or the first steps toward the heroin habit. (As illustrated in Appendix B, you could add the title of the appropriate category to each note card for ease in sorting them.) Reading through your note cards several times gives you a clear picture of your raw material and may uncover new relationships calling for new categories. For example, sifting through the cards may reveal a contrast between the viewpoints of popular and scholarly writers. If that contrast rests on differing interpretations of data or on different data, it may become a major section of your paper even though you never dreamed of that category at the start of your project.

As we suggested earlier, put the data on note cards to facilitate analysis. When you create and change categories, shuffle the cards to suit. In fact, the shuffling itself encourages creative insights. To break confining assumptions about how your information should fit, shuffle all the data like an oversize deck of cards. After a fair mixing, go through the new order watching for original and significant relationships. Perhaps a card on circumstances surrounding the arrest of addicts follows one on the social habits of addicts; combine the two pieces into a new category covering the problems of the addict who tries to blend with "normal" society to escape detection.

Considering and reconsidering the note cards strengthens your grasp of the information and choice of categories. The rough outline then arranges the categories. By arranging the cards within the basic categories to emphasize the most important and illustrative pieces of information, quotes, or opinions, you are on your way to the rough draft. Cards with weak or irrelevant information go in a "refuse" heap—out of the way but still reclaimable if you change your mind. This selection and reordering usually continues even as you write the report because the writing itself is a process of continual analysis to ensure the most accurate and vivid rendering of your experience.

The evaluation of data gathered by questionnaires or interviews also depends on classification techniques. In constructing your questionnaire or planning your interviews, you predicted the kinds of information necessary for a test of each hypothesis (Chapter Five and Appendix C). But the final data can be interrelated in a variety of ways beyond those that specifically apply to the hypotheses. For example, a study testing the notion that sports car enthusiasts are materialists would obviously include questions to define degrees of "materialism." In addition, questions might develop other information that might illuminate the thesis. Family income, personal income, education, age, sex, marital and family status, length of time interested in sports cars, length of time driving sports cars—these and other variables could interweave in several interesting patterns.

As you have seen from the various examples so far, it is not unusual to identify more than one variable in a term paper topic. The two main categories of variables most often used to describe a relationship are *dependent* and *independent*. The dependent variable is the one of primary interest, the one whose variation is to be the focus of the research. Its variance is explained in terms of the independent variable or variables. Take a look at one of our hypotheses from Chapter Three: Students who are very religious will drink less beer than students who are not very religious. The point of this hypothesis is to test the influence of the degree of religiosity on the amount of beer consumed by students. Here the dependent variable is amount of beer consumed; the independent variable is degree of religiosity. Now try the one with three variables: Students who drink excessively will have more academic problems and fewer friendships than moderate student drinkers. There are two dependent variables—amount of academic problem and number of friendships. The independent variable is degree of alcohol use. A variable may be defined as independent in one study and dependent in another. Complex studies may have several independent or dependent variables. One dependent variable and one independent variable are enough for most term paper projects. Because they can have many forms and can be combined in various ways, it is important to define them clearly. Now see if you can identify the variables in your thesis and hypotheses.

Association and Significance

Patterns form when two or more variables (e.g., income, age, cost of sports car) consistently vary together. The conventional name for this togetherness is "association." In a positive association, when one variable increases the other also increases. In a negative association, when one increases the other decreases. The higher the association, the stronger the indication that the two variables are in some way related. But even a perfect association does not indicate how they are related. Most importantly, association does not indicate whether one variable causes the other. An obvious example may clarify both what association is and why it does not establish cause and effect. If the increase in the number of books in a college library almost exactly parallels the increase in parking spaces in campus parking lots, the association would be highly positive. But no one would seriously believe that buying books creates parking spaces or vice-versa. If the statistics had shown that parking spaces disappear as books pile up, the association would be negative—but of course it still would not show cause and effect.

Both positive and negative associations show trends or patterns and thus can be significant to your study. The researcher working on the religious zeal of college students, for example, hypothesized a high negative association between time in college and church attendance. He expected his data to show that the churchgoing of students decreased as their years in college increased. The reasoning was that college causes the drop in religious zeal by encouraging the student to doubt. Testing the validity of the explanation is a separate task from establishing the association.

Be cautious about "proving" causal relationships as it is the most difficult task of social analysis. This step trips many researchers. You can seek clues and insights that will move you toward a closer understanding of your subject. For example, the student noting a drop in religious zeal might consider alternative explanations. One way of testing an alternate explanation of cause would be to examine other relationships. Perhaps the churches fail to offer the experiences that would involve most unmarried youth. Interviewing a control group—a group matched with college students in every way except college attendance—might show that zeal declines as age increases from eighteen to twenty-one. That finding would suggest that the argument about college studies needs more thought.

On finding two variables that co-vary (positively or negatively) you should immediately ask, "Are these really related?" The best way to answer that question is to see what happens when a third variable is added. If you already have data on additional variables, check their effects. (See Appendix E.) Don't give up if your data doesn't include the necessary variables—your incisive speculation can set the reader thinking.

Suppose you discover a strong negative relation between parents' wealth and college students' grades (Table 1, which is fictitious). You may be tempted to conclude that money corrupts scholarship. But consider such things as the admissions requirements of the college, the intelligence of the students, or their educational backgrounds. Perhaps students who are both bright and wealthy tend to go to another university, while only those who lacked money, brains or both enter the college you study. Using some measure of ability may show that the original relationship is "spurious," or unreal. Table 2 (also fictitious) shows that the relation of parental income to GPA vanishes when we bring I.Q. into the picture.

TABLE 1

Grade Point Average—by Parental Income
(Fictitious Data)

Parental Income

		$20,000 & over	Below $20,000
	A & B	20	80
GPA			
	C & Below	80	20
	Total	100	100

TABLE 2

Grade Point Average—by Parental Income and Students' I.Q.
(Fictitious Data)

		High I.Q. Parental Income		Low I.Q. Parental Income	
		$20,000 & over	Below $20,000	$20,000 & over	Below $20,000
	A & B	20	80	0	0
GPA					
	C & below	0	0	80	20
	Total	20	80	80	20

The original relationship is wiped out by the additional variable. This "wiping out" (rarely so complete as in the example) is called "explanation" or "interpretation." (A technical note: "explanation" refers to the effects of a variable that is antecedent to the correlated variables; "interpretation" refers to the effects of a variable that intervenes between them.)

You should also be alert for chances to clarify the relationship. For example, you may wonder if the relation of wealth and grades in Table 1 is due to a group of wealthy students—and wonder further about a hidden difference—maybe between males and females. The answer to that speculation appears in Table 3.

TABLE 3

Grade Point Average by Parental Income and Students' Sex
(Fictitious Data)

		Males		Females	
		Parental Income			
		$20,000 & over	Below $20,000	$20,000 & over	Below $20,000
GPA	A & B	0	40	20	40
	C & below	50	10	30	10
	Total	50	50	50	50

This table clarifies the original relationship, revealing that although parental income is related to grades for both sexes, the relation is far more striking for males. In sociology the search for precise information about a relationship is called "specification." *Explanation, interpretation,* and *specification* all refer to techniques that can become highly complex and revealing in professional analysis. But even their basic application within your limited time and resources can be helpful.

Up to this point we have talked as if your findings are simply to be accepted as "valid facts"—as accurate reflections of differences that really exist. Before accepting them as such, we should ask a few questions. Are you sure your sample is truly representative? That your questions didn't prejudice the respondent? Did you ask the right questions? Of course, by the analysis, you've passed the time to safeguard against sample and question distortion. No doubt you did that before you started. Now you compare your intentions against your results. Report frankly any biases you've discovered and don't forget them in the discussion of your findings. We hope that our suggestions in Chapter Five have minimized such unpleasant discoveries.

The Simplest Statistics

The basic devices of statistics are easy to use and understand. A *frequency distribution* simply totals the number of times some characteristic appears among the individuals in your group. How many students have grade point averages above C? How many have I.Q.s under 100? Over 140? How many drink beer? How many smoke marijuana? Finding the frequency is usually a step toward another measure, but it can be valuable in itself. Finding out how many students in a class were unable to buy an out-of-stock text helps the instructor place an accurate second order. Knowing the number of students graduating from high school influences the fall offerings in colleges. The number of new cars sold in the U.S. is a popular measure, along with the Gross National Product, of the state of the nation.

The most useful combination of figures is a *ratio* (or *relative frequency*). Ratios are simply proportions, so that "100 of the 200 persons interviewed owned cars" translates "one-half of those sampled" or "one out of two" or "fifty percent." In our society, we are so used to thinking of "most" or "the majority" as significant that we tend to ignore important considerations in using percents. Thus "most sports car owners" prepares us for a significant finding. But significance is a relative thing. Knowing that "15 percent of sports car drivers entered a fourth of their rallies after drinking a third of a fifth of 40 percent alcohol (80 proof) whiskey" would make drivers as well as insurance underwriters shudder. The significance of a particular percentage depends partly on what you know about the population and what is important to it. If twenty percent of the students in a political science course refused to take a final exam as a political protest, would you consider that proportion important? Would the protest be a "pathetic" or a "dramatic" showing?

Sometimes a frequency is significant even though it is "ridiculously" small. For example, surveys of persons who inhale or inject substances for "kicks" usually turn up one or two who shoot plain water into their veins. Statistically they may be insignificant, but their very existence is striking. Sometimes a frequency is significant *because* it is small. For example, a sociologist in a "dry" community found that only a few persons were in favor of the ban on liquor sales—yet almost everyone thought that "most" of his neighbors favored the ban. This suggested, contrary to common sense political wisdom, that votes could be won by talking against the ban. Discovering a low frequency thus aided a political victory and increased understanding of voting behavior.

Another valuable ratio is the *mean*, or the calculated average. It shows a "central tendency"—that is, the tendency of the data to cluster around some midpoint. Imagine a campus where all students are so well-heeled they drive new sports cars. For these cars, a sample twenty students paid $3,000, ten paid $4,000 and another twenty paid $5,000. The average price (the mean price) is easy to calculate:

$$\frac{(20 \times 3,000) + (10 \times 4,000) + (20 \times 5,000)}{50} =$$

$$\frac{60,000 + 40,000 + 100,000}{50} = \frac{200,000}{50} = \$4,000$$

The problem is that clustered numbers have queer effects on the mean. If forty owners paid $125 each for what might be called sports cars, while ten shelled out $19,500 each for an Aston-Martin, Lamborghini or Ferrari, the mean price would be $4,000—the same as the first campus! The mean, then, can be misleading. Use it with care.

The *mode* represents the item or figure appearing most often. In the second example of sports car prices, the mode is $125. The first example has two modes, $3,000 and $5,000.

The *median* points to the center of your data. To find it, arrange the items in order of frequency, from the least to the most. Then count halfway up or down the list of figures. The value of the central case is the median. Again using the first example of sports car prices, we find that, counting either up or down, the twenty-fifth case is $3,000. In the second example the median is $125. Usually the mean suits your purpose, but check it against the median and mode to see that a strange distribution hasn't thrown you off. Keep in mind that even simple statistical tools require careful use.

Statistics and Critical Thinking

Statistical analysis can shake down a confusing mass of numbers into a concise index for interpretation. Careful statistical analysis involves complicated techniques to evaluate the accuracy and reliability of results. If you want to explore some of these more complex methods, we include a few in Appendix F. But the apparent precision of calculation should not lead to their slavish use. Statistical tests can't definitely prove your hypotheses; the statistics may come from a mistaken survey or your application of them may be unjustified. But they present evidence persuasively.

Be especially careful applying statistics developed by others. In the following passage, the student uses such evidence without realizing (or at least without explaining) that the data could support other interpretations.

"In Detroit and Chicago, three-fourths of the persons arrested for such crimes were Negroes." Mere bouts with the law indicating lower moral values are substantiated by statistics on black family life. While only 3.07 percent of white births were illegitimate in 1963, 23.59 percent of black births were. While only 8.6 percent of white families were headed by women in 1960, 23.2 percent of black families were. The family seems the backbone of the white community; this indication of black family breakdown definitely represents a lower moral conduct standard.

Another student, however, set his findings in a context to explain that the significance of his results depends on fitting the complexities of life into understandable concepts.

I think it would be difficult to reach perfectly valid conclusions because of the intangibility of *faith*. Faith and devotion cannot be measured like the number of weekly cocktail parties in Park Forest or the number of people who voted for Goldwater in 1964. Religion is personal, and, although general trends can be disclosed, it is hard to obtain exact descriptions of intangible senses. The spiritual human element is too deeply involved here.

Research is the hope that categorizing data will help us grapple with that complexity. But the best analysis comes from an honest, perceptive examination of the problem and your relevant information. Though the term paper must depend on limited data, it provides plenty of space for you to consider thoughtfully your predispositions, theses, hypotheses, methods, and results.

Analyzing

The

Report

The look of some professional articles in sociology may have implied that you should adopt a special reporting style. Certainly the report must logically and objectively present evidence, methods, and conclusions, but that can be done as many ways as there are writers. You may use special terms, statistics, and footnotes, but these are secondary elements to the basic explanation of your approach and results. Within a basic framework we expect you to follow a pattern best suited to your talent and topic, so most of our comments are suggestions, not rules. Of course your instructor may have special requirements, so be alert to anything he or she specifies that we make optional or fail to mention.

Approach the report with the resolve—and the time—to write at least two drafts. Each revision increases the chance that your reader will actually grasp what you intend to say. An outline helps start the rough draft, but don't let it run away with itself. Outline to clarify your basic points and what leads up to them, then let the rough draft roll. This draft will clarify your ideas and put your research in perspective. The time to cut, add, and rearrange is later, so plough through the first draft without imagining that someone is looking over your shoulder and frowning at clumsy sentences. As Hemingway said, the only important thing about a first draft is that it gets done. So take the reader seriously into account when you revise. That's the time to test sentences, checking to make sure that transitions really connect your turns of mind and that what seems obvious to you will be clear to the reader.

Starting to Write

A good start for the rough draft is a blunt statement of your basic idea for the project. "Blunt," not concise and precise. Save the struggle for the perfect first sentence and paragraph for the final draft. Here is an example of a beginning beginning: "I am going to try to explain how I got involved with my study on bias against women in housing, how I went about it, and my conclusion that there was some bias against single women students who tried to find apartments near campus."

It's wordy, but the writer's pencil, pen, or typewriter is moving. The statement outlines the areas for explanation and can lead to a fairly detailed outline.

Thesis: There is bias against women in housing.

Hypothesis 1: Single women students will be refused apartments more often than will single men students.

Hypothesis 2: Single women students will have to pay more rent than will single men students for equivalent apartments.

    I. Procedures for testing hypotheses
        A. Library research
        B. Field research
            1. Choosing samples
            2. Gathering data
                a. Short interview schedule for students
                b. Short questionnaire for landlords/managers
                c. Pretests

The Report

II. Problems in testing hypotheses
  A. Library
    1. Information on single persons not broken down by sex
    2. New ideas about controlling samples for marital and employment background
  B. Field
    1. Students
      a. Controls of looks
        1. Racial stereotypes
        2. Hair and clothing style
        3. Age
      b. Controls of background
        1. Past or future marriage tie
        2. Employment
    2. Landlords/managers
      a. Poor returns of questionnaire
      b. In-depth interviews with office managers of two rental agencies.
    3. Finding samples
      a. Information unavailable through dean's office
      b. Students contacted through classes
      c. Randomizing process for list of landlords/managers
III. Data
  A. Library
  B. Field
    1. Raw data
    2. Processed data
      a. Methods of processing
      b. Problems of processing
IV. Findings
  A. Hypothesis 1
  B. Hypothesis 2
 V. Conclusion
  A. Support for thesis
  B. Implications for further research
  C. Social significance

This outline shows a reasonable order of the major and minor aspects of research procedures. A more detailed outline would now be possible, one that would show every fact, idea, quote, or example that the writer wanted to use in the report. If you find such detailed outlines inhibiting, go directly to the rough draft. During revision you can insert the appropriate specifics from your notecards and data sheets.

Beginnings

A paper that followed the order of the outline could begin with a statement that would show the development of the topic and the writer's involvement.

Two months ago a friend of mine decided to live alone in an apartment near school. She had spent her first semester of college in a dorm, then shared an apartment with two other women during the second semester and the summer. She started looking for her own place in mid-August, which meant plenty of time to get established before classes started. We would meet nearly every evening, and she would tell me stories about her search. She met landlords who were either skeptical or negative, and a time or two she felt an apartment that was really vacant became unavailable when the landlord found out she was a student with no immediate plans for marriage. In talking over the cost, we thought inflated rents might be another way landlords discouraged her.

A time or two I offered to go back to the apartment house and see what the landlord's attitude would be, but we never got that idea into action. Then I started thinking about going along with her to see for myself. Again, we didn't do anything about it. When we started talking over my work in school, the term paper assignment hit both of us as a good way to combine our interests.

We started with the idea that she might be having trouble because she was a student. We then worked through different aspects of what her "problem" might be for the landlords: being single? young? a college student? I decided to focus on the woman's angle after talking with men in her position who had a different experience from hers in hunting apartments. I was especially interested as I might myself be looking into living alone one of these days.

The basic organization of these three paragraphs is chronological. This order fits this beginning because the writer's involvement rests on a chain of events that led naturally to the thesis. Chronological ordering is only one of many arrangements possible, but it is familiar and thus tempting. The danger is that it may turn the paper into a list of happenings connected by "then" and "next." Your experiences may interest the reader, but he's anxious to learn their point.

An alternative beginning is to get right to the point:

When a close friend of mine began to have trouble finding an apartment, I formed the tentative thesis that landlords and apartment managers are biased against women. To work this into a research project, I focused on further details of my friend's situation as single, a student, and age twenty. My test aspects of my hypotheses focused on the availability and the cost of apartments.

1) Single women students will be refused apartments more often than will single men students.
2) Single women students will have to pay more rent than will single men students for equivalent apartments.

The next paragraph might outline the field research, then lead into a paragraph on library work. This version focuses not on the researcher's process of involvement in the topic, as does the first one, but on the research as it helps to clarify a possible social phenomenon. Both would clearly report the same basic information but would represent two experiences of the term paper.

Endings

An ending simply draws the reader's attention to the main point established by your work. It may include reasonable speculation based on the necessarily limited scope of the research.

After completing my research, I began to wonder if bias against women might be related to the sex of managers and landlords. If most of controllers of rentals are men, as in my study, then the bias might be a general one related to resistance to the changing roles of women in our present society. Perhaps my friend is one of a group of women who are feeling the reaction of this resistance, and perhaps this reaction is only a temporary effect of the stress of a social transition. Once the independence of women becomes a fact of life, the pattern of bias may disappear.

Another style of ending draws the reader into considering directions for further research. Avoid the cliché, "my research is a beginning, but much work remains to be done." Instead, be specific about what another study might attempt.

My thesis that there is bias against women in housing was supported at least for single women students in my research. But my work indicated a need for more thorough control of factors like age, employment, and life-style. It may be that conservative, single women in their fifties find it easier to find housing than their male counterparts. Perhaps a study which focused on apartments far from the campus would show a different result. And perhaps another student in another semester would find my report a good jumping off place for a term paper project.

But don't get carried away. Endings that become ringing declarations or calls to action undermine the value of your data and your trustworthiness as a researcher.

> As my research has shown, bias against women in housing is part and parcel of a prejudice against females that permeates the entire fabric of American society. If women are truly to be guaranteed equality in the pursuit of happiness, certainly the place to start is with right to seek shelter on an equal footing with men. As an educational institution, this college should take the lead in our community by refusing to list housing controlled by landlords and managers who my study shows are biased. Perhaps law school students should take up the cause and aid in the prosecution of this latest attempt to deny the basic rights of one group of citizens.

Though this writer writes with conviction, the emotionally worded statements demand a proof far beyond the scope of the research. By imposing what appears to be a prior committment, the researcher prejudices evidence and conclusions that may be essentially sound.

Good beginnings and endings attract and reinforce the reader's interest, but without supporting details of the research they signify nothing. Select those decisions and experiences crucial to understanding your thesis, method, data, and conclusions. In preceding sections of this book we demonstrated that every stage of your research may be rich with questions, ideas, and choices; and nearly every decision can be considered significant for some reason. You have a lot of material to make the report vivid.

One student who surveyed faculty members included a brief explanation for the eleven open-ended questions which guided the interviews. Here are the first three:

> 1. *Why did you choose UCSB?* This was an easy first question, but it did reveal what the teacher looked for in a school, its location, how important the quality of the student body is, if weather influenced the decision, if a name school is important—all of this without the teacher being aware of the extra information he or she was giving.

2. *How were you first made to want to teach?* This proved a good question to watch the first reaction with because many teachers looked puzzled or said, "Wanted?—It was the only thing I could do with my interests," or, "I just ended up teaching!"

3. *How is teaching enjoyable to you?* This is a way of asking why do you teach without the insult of straightforwardness of the direct question. This leaves the teachers free to begin where they want, and they will generally begin with the most important reason to them.

Another student included relevant details from encounters with respondents to shed light on the low percentage of questionnaires returned.

> The extremely poor returns (roughly thirty percent) can at least partially be attributed to sensitivity. Even personal friends had to be reassured that the report was confidential. General suspiciousness was markedly evident; one suspecting person labeled my survey a "communist plot." Another thought the survey "too personal," and that I would get his name and address. Upon reassurance that his reply was entirely confidential he gruffly refused. I then offered him thirteen cents for a stamp and again he refused, stating that somehow I would still get his name and address and he disliked such surveys though he had been cooperative before discovering the subject. This latter view seemed to pervade many of those who even turned down the offer to take a survey home. These indications lead me to believe that the issue did, indeed, smite a suburban sore.

This passage is a model of paragraph construction as well as detail. Both the first and last sentences touch the point of the explanation, and the rest explain that point. Each paragraph should thus be a miniature report, with one of its sentences having the extra responsibility of linking that paragraph to another. Those links form a clear-cut path through the report. The first sentence of the student's next paragraph began, "Of the thirty percent who did return the questionnaire . . .," which picks up an element from the preceding paragraph to establish the link. It could also have begun, "This sensitivity" and thus led the reader in a different direction.

That effort to relate one piece of the report to another is especially important when using graphic aids such as tables and illustrations. Their purpose is to clarify your discussion, not replace it. The best place for each table, graph, or illustration is near its explanation in your text. However, if that becomes impossible, put them together in an appendix at the appropriate point in your discussion (e.g., "see Appendix B, Table 3"). If the table or illustration comes from an article or book, be sure to acknowledge the source. (But don't tear out such aids unless you own the source; the librarian can probably help you make a photocopy and save you from becoming a criminal in your reader's eyes!)

Style

Though an array of statistical tables and graphs may make a paper look professional, what really counts is the overall report—the discussion of your thesis and research. The report should communicate discoveries and frustrations along with data. It should be humane, but not sentimental; objective, but not lifeless. Acting as a dispassionate guide, you point out the landmarks of your own research. Write vividly (i.e., with life), but restrain passionate appeals to your reader's judgment. Objectivity requires suspended judgment—a mind open to more than one solution to a problem.

A mistaken attempt at "objective writing" systematically uses passive constructions that take the life out of sentences without really changing the writer's responsibility for the information. "It was found that" is a passive construction that means "I found that," just as does "this writer found that." The first and last are pathetic attempts of the writer to appear objective, as only the most naive reader could imagine that waving a wand over the phrasing changes the source of information. "I" is straightforward and thus preferable to the other phrasings. Of course if the information isn't yours, the reader expects you to acknowledge the source (e.g., "Michner found that").

Lively writing requires something more, however, than straightforwardly repeating "I." Your information and insights directly stated give the paper its attraction. For example, suppose your rough draft had this sentence: "It was found by this writer from his data that churchgoing had declined by twenty-five percent in the freshman year." The wording could be: "I found that churchgoing had dropped . . ." But it could just as easily be: "Churchgoing had dropped. . ." Without a footnote or similar acknowledgement of debt, the information must come from you. (It better not have come from your imagination, so "from his data" is unnecessary.) The emphasis properly shifts from "I" to what makes "I" interesting—your discovery. Note how smoothly this student explores a possibility without using "I":

> It would have been possible to alleviate some of these problems by lengthening the questionnaire and cutting down its scope. But this in turn would have probably made it harder to handle, decreased the number of responses and in turn meant cutting out some of the important factors.

Sometimes "my" constructions can effectively replace "I." Consider this sequence: "I started my questionnaire by asking"; "My questionnaire started by asking"; "My first question was"; "The questionnaire began with." But occasionally "I" is best and least strained, so don't automatically eliminate every single one.

Inventing your own terms to describe special features of the topic is one way to identify your writings; but too many new terms irritate rather than aid your reader. Define any special terms briefly and precisely at their first occurrence in your report (not in a list that the reader must consult before continuing to read). Here is a good example of what *not* to do:

> I have used *socially mobile* and *upwardly mobile*. Hence for the purpose of this paper I define the two as being identically equal. Therefore, the term *social mobility* refers to *upward mobility*.

First, the passage is inefficient; thirty-two words do the work of ten. ("In my paper social mobility and upward mobility are synonymous.") Second, if the words are synonymous why use both? Third, the terms remain undefined, referring to nothing except each other. Though we could guess at their meaning, the point of special terms is to eliminate guesswork. Perhaps this rewording better defines the writer's idea:

> In this paper *socially mobile* means that the freedom to move into a higher social class depends on achievement rather than background. In America white, Anglo-Saxon Protestants are socially mobile because none of these social characteristics restricts their ambition. Jews are less socially mobile because certain achievements are impossible for them simply because of their religion; and blacks are severely restricted by their color.

The examples could be left out without damage to the basic definition, but that depends on how much the writer thinks the reader needs them.

Another aspect of style that depends on the relation of writer and reader is the appropriate degree of formality. This manual, for example, stretches the limits of traditional textbook style in an effort to stimulate your interest in a term paper. We use contractions along with the "you" and "we" of direct address. Quite legitimately, however, we suggest that you do as we say, not as we do. Our style is too informal for a term paper. Because we actually recommend action, the "you" fits. But you are simply reporting, which requires an objective tone. Contractions imply a social equality—one friend advising another—and thus are probably out of place if your relationship with your reader is formal.

Rely on detail, precision, conciseness, and active constructions to make your writing effective. We have given several examples of these virtues already, but perhaps a brief catalog here will help put them in your power.

ACTIVE

Passive: It was stated by Henry Glibbton that . . .

Active: Henry Glibbton wrote . . .
According to Henry Glibbton . . .

Passive: The student was observed copying figures from his shirt pocket.

Active: I saw the student copy figures from his shirt pocket.
One student saw another copy . . .
The student copied . . .

DETAILED

General: The student cheated.

Detailed: The student copied figures from a sheet hidden in his shirt pocket.

General: The respondent refused the questionnaire because he didn't approve of it.

Detailed: The respondent refused the questionnaire because he objected to answering "prying" questions about his religion.

PRECISE

Vague: The respondents were influenced by the length of the questionnaire.

Precise:	The respondents complained that the questionnaire was too long.
Vague:	He had regular contact with marijuana.
Precise:	He smoked marijuana regularly. (*Detailed*: "He smoked two or three marijuana cigarettes a week.")

CONCISE

Wordy:	I am going to present some evidence to show that the group placed a high value on education at colleges located in the East.
Concise:	The group prized an Ivy League education.
Wordy:	I had mailed out 250 questionnaires and most of them were sent to students in the senior class who were living in dorms.
Concise (and Precise):	I sent 175 of the 250 questionnaires to seniors living in dorms.

Enough time for revision can make improving your sentences almost a game. Almost. For example, eliminating wordiness can be played as a search for essentials.

Directions: 1) In an awkward sentence underline the words that carry the message.
2) Arrange these words in a sensible order.
3) Add the fewest words necessary to make a decent English sentence.
4) Improve it.

Example:
1) I had mailed out 250 questionnaires and most of them were sent to students in the senior class who were living in dorms.
2) Most 250 questionnaires mailed students senior dorms.
3) Most of the 250 questionnaires were mailed to seniors living in dorms.
4) Of the 250 questionnaires, I sent 175 to seniors living in dorms, and the other 75 to seniors living in college-owned rooming houses.

The Report

All these improvements follow your first draft, which should be a spontaneous outpouring of ideas and information with little heed to organization and less to sentence refinement. A tentative outline helps start the rough draft, and the rough draft reveals your weak points. Revise by keeping the point of your paper clearly in mind—even pasted on the wall above your desk. And alongside it might be Hemingway's concise motto: *Easy writing makes hard reading.*

The Report

The
Format

A few scholarly devices ornament good research and writing; they trim your paper to fit neatly into the academic tradition. Some of these matters can follow several models, and your instructor usually specifies a choice. Conventions of quotation and paraphrase (Appendix B) are traditionally fixed. Being perfect in these matters won't justify poor research or writing, but acknowledging the work of others accurately and clearly will reinforce the basic value of your paper.

The most physical matters are the most minor and the most rapidly summarized. Make your typewriting crisp and black, which may mean investing in a new ribbon. Margins should be wide enough to encourage the instructor's marginal commentary. (Allow 1 inch at the right, top and bottom, but 1 ¾ inches at the edge that's bound.) Double space your text. Number the pages. The title page should include the title of your paper, your name, the instructor's name, the number and section of the course, and the date. Correct typing errors with a pen, but retype a page that is so peppered with errors it looks like a rough draft. You might choose an "erasable" paper, but avoid extremely thin paper, the kind that feels like skin and reveals the lines of one page between the lines of the page above it. Make a carbon copy for yourself to avoid heartbreak if the instructor's copy should disappear before he or she reads it—or if the instructor wants to keep it as a model of imagination and technique.

Most of a library paper, and perhaps some of a field research paper, will be paraphrase and quotation. Document quotations but also facts and ideas developed by others. (See Appendix B for details of quotation and paraphrase.) Footnotes, textual documentation, and bibliography show your reader the who, where, and when of your sources so the information can be evaluated and perhaps retrieved. Several forms exist for such reference, and your instructor may have something particular in mind. Our examples follow two of the simplest variations within the two most popular forms. Be consistent in using whatever style you choose.

Footnoting

As the term suggests, a footnote traditionally appears at the foot of the page that includes the material footnoted. Because that takes a little juggling in a typewritten paper, many instructors permit footnotes to be gathered on one or two pages at the end of the paper (preceding the bibliography). It works a little hardship on the reader but considerably eases the writer's task. To simplify the reader's task, number the footnotes consecutively through the paper (instead of starting each page with "1"). We recommend another, more significant, simplification in your footnotes: eliminate Latin abbreviations. The dangers in this simplification are: 1) angering your reader, and 2) losing the ability to read these abbreviations in the work of others. To minimize the latter, we provide a little guide to translation in our examples. The former is up to you. Observe the examples carefully to note the information given, its order, and its punctuation.

Books

[4]Joseph A. Kahl, The American Class Structure (New York: Rine-

hart & Co., Inc., 1959), p. 223. [The first reference to a source gives full information.]

⁵Kahl, p. 223. [This abbreviation could be ⁵Loc cit.]

⁶Kahl, p. 225. [Could be ⁶Ibid., p. 225.]

⁷Philip E. Jacob, Changing Values in College (New Haven: Hazel Foundation, 1956), p. 58.

⁸Kahl, p. 225. [Could be ⁸Kahl, op. cit., p. 225.]

⁹Jacob, Changing Values, p. 61. [Add a short title when your paper includes two works by the same author.]

Periodicals

¹⁰P. D. Bardis, "Religiosity Among Jewish Students in a Metropolitan University," Sociology and Social Research, Vol. 49 (October 1964), pp. 91-92. [Could be the same but with abbreviated journal title and volume in Roman numerals: Sociol. & Soc. Res., XLIX (October 1964), 91-92.]

¹¹John Cogley, "Most Students Are Conventional, Professor Says," The New York Times, October 10, 1975, p. 4. [The title is the story's headline.]

Unpublished Sources

¹²Bryan A. Smith, The Study of Sociology, a ditto (from Mr. Smith's Sociology 101 class, Section 2, Fall 1975, Seymour Williams College), p. 2.

¹³Interview with Bryan A. Smith (Associate Professor of Sociology, Seymour Williams College), November 9, 1975.

A Source with More than Three Authors

¹⁴Edmund G. Williamson and others, A Study of Participation in College Activities (Minneapolis: University of Minnesota, 1954), p. 24. [Could also be Edmund G. Williamson, et al., with the rest the same.]

Works with Author Unknown or Not Listed

[15]"Survey of the Political and Religious Attitudes of American College Students," National Review, Vol. 15 (October 8, 1963), p. 280.

Works Produced by an Organization

[16]Harvard University Student Council, Religion at Harvard (Cambridge: Harvard University Press, 1956), p. 37.

Items from a Collection

[17]Talcott Parsons, "A Revised Analytical Approach to the Theory of Social Stratification," Class, Status and Power: A Reader in Social Stratification, eds. Reinhard Bendix and Seymour Martin Lipset (Glencoe, Ill.: The Free Press, 1953), p. 128.

Translated Sources

[18]Karl Mannheim, Ideology and Utopia: An Introduction to the Sociology of Knowledge, trans. Louis Wirth and Edward Shils (New York: Harcourt, Brace and Co., 1936), p. 31.

Explanatory Footnotes

The explanatory or content footnote allows you to include information that is out of place in the text. Because it fragments the reader's attention, use sparingly.

[19]Twenty-six respondents had apparently erased their first answer to this question. But I could not make out their first answers, nor could I work up any interpretation for the erasures.

The sample page reproduced opposite shows how footnote numbers in the text correspond to the footnotes. Both the text and footnotes are fictional.

The Format

road to independence and middle-class security. To decide between these alternatives would require another questionnaire controlling the variables of money and time.[4]

Some support for the thesis that sophisticated students want more than conventional educations comes from a study of students in ten American graduate schools. These students were to construct an ideal graduate curriculum and to answer this question: "Should graduate study involve work at more than one university? Explain."

Sixty-five percent of the students who answered yes had attended more than one college on the way to a B.A.[5] No information was available on the family incomes of the students polled, but three-fourths of those answering yes were self-supporting in graduate school.[6] Despite the financial sacrifice in graduate school, they were willing to risk the simplicity of working at one school for the broader experience of two. As John A. Tarle, a professor of sociology at Wheeler University, observed, ". . . [I] have been grateful more than once that each campus gave me a new point of view."[7]

---

[4]Sample question: How interested would you be in spending a year at a different college if costs were the same to you as at this campus?

[5]Ivan C. O'Neill, "Students Create the Ideal Graduate Program," American Review of Higher Education, Vol. 60 (Spring 1975), p. 23.

[6]O'Neill, p. 25.

[7]The Student and His Education (New York: The Academic Press, 1961), p. 152. [*Note that the footnote omits information supplied in the text—in this case the author's name.*]

Textual Documentation

Another style of documentation places the author's last name, the date of his work, and the page number within parentheses after the reference to the work in your text. This style keeps the reader's attention on your text yet immediately supplies both with the name and date, which give the reader a means to judge the source. Take a look at the sample page of text again, this time noting the differences in the second paragraph.

-3-

road to independence and middle-class security. To decide between these alternatives would require another questionnaire controlling the variables of money and time.*

Some support for the thesis that sophisticated students want more than conventional educations comes from a study of students in ten American graduate schools. These students were to construct an ideal graduate curriculum and were asked this question: "Should graduate study involve work at more than one university? Explain."

Sixty-five percent of the students who answered yes had attended more than one college on the way to a B.A. (O'Neill, 1975: 23). No information was available on the family incomes of the students polled, but three-fourths of those answering yes were self-supporting in graduate school (O'Neill, 1975: 25). Despite the financial sacrifice in graduate school, they still were willing to risk the simplicity of working at one school for the broader experience of two. As John A. Tarle (1961a:152), a professor of sociology at Wheeler University, observed, ". . . [I] have been grateful more than once that each campus gave me a new point of view." [*Note that "1961a" means that the list of references has another item Tarle published that year.*]

---

*Sample question: How interested would you be in spending a year at a different college if costs were the same to you as at this campus?

The form shown in our example page follows the style of the *American Sociological Review,* the official journal of the American Sociological Association. The style for the *American Journal of Sociology* has yet another pattern, though similar to this one. For both journals, the first page of each issue gives the forms for citation and reference. Be sure to consult a recent issue, as these forms are revised from time to time. (To see the limits your instructor has to meet to publish an article in either of these journals, take a look at the requirements for contributors that appear along with the examples for citation and reference.)

The main difference between textual and footnote citations is that the former elevates the references to the text and abbreviates all of them. But remember that only the first references in footnotes give full information; the subsequent abbreviations, just as in textual documentation, require the reader to look elsewhere for the full story on a source.

Bibliography or List of References

The "elsewhere" your reader must look is the end of your paper where an alphabetical list of the research materials you found especially valuable in writing the paper can be found. It includes all the references cited in your text plus those that influenced you more generally. To restrain students from padding this list, an instructor will sometimes restrict the bibliography to references cited in the text. Listing them alphabetically on a separate page (or pages) at the back of the paper means that a reader puzzled by an abbreviated reference can flip to the end and locate the full information at a glance. The following examples show some details of the arrangement of sources corresponding to footnote or textual documentation. Note especially how bibliography listings differ in arrangement and punctuation from footnote listings.

BIBLIOGRAPHY
[Corresponds to a sample of our footnotes]

Bardis, P. D. "Religiosity Among Jewish Students in a Metropolitan University," Sociology and Social Research, Vol. 49 (October 1964), pp. 90-95. [The page numbers include the whole article.]

Harvard University Student Council. Religion at Harvard. Cambridge, Mass.: Harvard University Press, 1956.

Kahl, Joseph A. The American Class Structure. New York: Rinehart & Co., Inc., 1959.

O'Neill, Ivan C. "Students Create the Ideal Graduate Program," American Review of Higher Education, Vol. 60 (Spring 1975), pp. 20-24.

Smith, Bryan A. Associate Professor of Sociology, Seymour Williams College. Interview, November 9, 1975.

"Survey of the Political and Religious Attitudes of American College Students," National Review, Vol. 15 (October 8, 1963), pp. 279-302.

Tarle, John A. The Student and His Education. New York: The Academic Press, 1961.

Tarle, John A. "Wandering Academics," Journal of Graduate Education, Vol. 41 (Fall 1961), pp. 44-52.

Wilson, Francis P. and others. A Study of College Roles. Chicago: Minerva Press, 1975.

The following list of references follows the style of the *American Sociological Review* and corresponds to the citations in our sample pages.

REFERENCES

[Corresponds to a sample of our textual documentation]

Bardis, P.D.
1964   "Religiosity among Jewish students in a metropolitan university." Sociology and Social Research 49:90-95.

Harvard University Student Council
1956   Religion at Harvard. Cambridge, Mass.: Harvard.

Kahl, Joseph A.
1959   The American Class Structure. New York: Rinehart.

O'Neill, Ivan C.
1975   "Students create the ideal graduate pro-
                       gram." American Review of Higher Educa-
                       tion 60:20-24.

Smith, Bryan A.
1975   Associate Professor of Sociology, Seymour
                       William College. Interview: November 9.

"Survey of the political and religious attitudes of American college
1963   students." National Review 15:279-302.

Tarle, John A.
1961   The Student and His Education. New York:
                       Academic.

Tarle, John A.
1961b   "Wandering academics." Journal of Gradu-
                       ate Studies 41:44-52.

Wilson, Francis P., Bruce Charlton, Jr., and Tor Denton
1975   A Study of College Roles. Chicago: Minerva.

If they are new to you, both documentation and bibliography may seem a wilderness of detail. By keeping a few basic principles in mind, you can fit your information to the patterns in our examples.

1. The bibliography listing points to the whole source—the whole book or the whole article; the footnote or textual documentation points to a specific page from the source.

2. Information for the bibliography comes entirely from your bib cards; the footnote or textual documentation requires the basic "locate" information from the bib card plus the page number from the note card.

3. If your source doesn't fit one of our patterns, use your good sense to list the information similarly.

If you would like to wade deeper into the problems of format, refer to one of the following sources.

Cooper, Charles W. and Edward J. Robins. *The Term Paper: A Manual and Model.* 4th ed. Stanford: Stanford University Press, 1967.

Lester, James D. *Writing Research Papers: A Complete Guide*. 2nd ed. Glenview, Ill.: Scott, Foresman and Co., 1975.

The MLA Style Sheet. 2nd ed. New York: Modern Language Association of America, 1970.

Piper, James. *Piper's Guide to Research*. Encino, Calif.: Dickenson, 1972.

Publication Manual of the American Psychological Association. 2nd ed. Washington, D.C.: American Psychological Association, 1974.

Turabian, Kate L. *A Manual for Writers of Term Papers, Theses and Dissertations*. 4th ed. Chicago: The University of Chicago Press, 1973.

The Format

Tips on Library Research

The Bibliography Card

The following sample bib cards demonstrate the evolution of research from the checking of indexes (or bibliographies) to the skimming of sources to see which merit thorough reading. (Remember that the information from thorough reading goes on note cards.)

Take the time to spell titles just as they appear instead of using your own abbreviations; it will save confusion later when you try to decide if "soc" means social, society, or sociology.

Taken from the list of sources in this manual.

> Oppenheim, A. N. *Questionnaire Design and Attitude Measurement*
> New York: Basic Books, Inc.
> 1966
> Good list of sources.
>   march 1st — checked
>   "   20th. — rechecked

Information taken from a bibliography listing.

If the book isn't in your library, the date will help you check a book review for a source that looks important.

> Mills, C. Wright. *The Sociological Imagination*,
> New York: Oxford Univ. Press, 1959.

Call number found in card catalog [the example shows a Library of Congress call number].

> Mills, C. Wright. *The Sociological Imagination*,
> New York: Oxford Univ. Press, 1959
> H
> 61
> M5

Contents and index skimmed for relevant information.

> Mills, C. Wright. *The Sociological Imagination*,
> New York: Oxford Univ. Press, 1959
> H
> 61   Comprehensive analysis of sociology.
> M5   Interesting commentary on
>   academic cliques (pp. 107-113).
>   maybe recheck.

Information from an index.

Both volume number and year are valuable; if one should be misprinted, the other locates the source.

Gilliland, adam R. "Change in Religious Beliefs of College Students"
J. Soc. Psy., Vol. 37 (1953), pp. 113-116.

Name spelled out and location added.

Gilliland, adam R. "Change in Religious Beliefs of College Students"
Bound on open Shelves   J. Soc. Psy., Vol 37 (1933), pp 113-116.
(Journal of Social Psychology)

Gilliland, adam R. "Change in Religious Beliefs of College Students
Bound on open Shelves   J. Soc. Psy., Vol. 37 (1953), pp. 113-116 (Journal of Social Psychology)

Skimmed for future careful readings.

Excellent! Specific, right on the topic. Recheck.

The Note Card

To demonstrate both the variety of notes possible and the way they work into a term paper, we created a passage from a source article, drew out information and opinions, and then worked them into a new form.

questionnaires handed out as the bus started for the stadium. A pretest group had received the questionnaires after the game, but many refused to complete them either because of excessively low or excessively high spirits, depending on the outcome of the game. Pencils supplied with the questionnaires given to the study group bore the team's name and color. The respondents could keep the pencils—and they did, often saying, "It's for the kid." Collecting the questionnaires as the bus approached the stadium netted a good return—usually 90 percent; the mild social pressure of the group (seeing one another "working") no doubt helped achieve this high figure.

Of the 506 in the sample, over 75 percent (400) had never attended college. Table 2 gives the breakdown according to years of education and shows that these faithful supporters at least identify with a university team. To get at the source of this support, we first found out the circumstances leading the supporter to buy his ticket. We then asked him why he attended the games and what he "got out of" the afternoons spent this way. We had expected a high percentage to be recruited by ticket salesmen (who were perhaps their bosses at work) but found that nearly 60 percent had themselves reserved the season ticket. One respondent penciled, "I remind Joey to sell me a ticket." Possibly the very act of buying a ticket expresses a conviction for these fans and thus strengthens their identification with the university. The reasons

Note Cards

Author's last name
—easy to match
with bib card.

A blank space here signals
a forgotten page number

Fact + your
opinion

Felton and Richards   p. 25
400 of 506 (75%+) bussed football supporters had no college
(good table, but very detailed)

Library Research

Quote (researcher's opinion + fact)

> Felton and Richards   p. 25
>
> Bussed football supporters returning questionnaires.
>
> "... the mild social pressure of the group (seeing one another working") no doubt helped achieve this high figure." (90% return)

Paraphrase (researcher's opinion + fact)

> Felton and Richards   p. 25
>
> Researchers speculate that bussed football fans identify with the college (although 73% have never attended) because they buy tickets in advance.

Analysis (your opinion)

> Felton and Richards   p. 25
>
> The authors make no comment on the possible bias involved in a respondent's being surrounded by a bus-full of other fans:
> 1) he might feel disloyal unless his answers support team supporters
> 2) he might up his income and education levels

Later, when arranging the cards according to the development of your paper, you might add a short reference to the part of the paper the card supports.

Library Research

Felton and Richards
    Method
p. 25

Bussed football supporters return-
ing questionnaires

"... the mild social pressure of
the group (seeing one another"working") no doubt helped achieve this
high figure." (90% return)

Your Paper

Quotation (worked in as part of sentence; brackets enclose your insertions)

-4-

pointed to a possible device for surveying football fans. The researchers passed out questionnaires to bus-loads of fans before they arrived at the game. Not only did the survey get them at a peak of enthusiasm, but "the mild social pressure of the group (seeing one another 'working') no doubt helped achieve this high figure [a 90 percent return]."[6] Though the researchers didn't mention a "proc-

Paraphrase

-5-

We also wanted to check fans who held season tickets, because Felton and Richards suggested that buying a ticket in advance illustrates an identification with the college.[8] Consequently, the fans they reported that 75 percent of their sample of football supporters bussed to games had no college.[10] Similar findings in a study of audiences regularly watching a college quiz-bowl TV show had no

Note that only three of the four notes appeared in the paper; and that's a high percentage because we're trying to show briefly several kinds of notes in several contexts.

The following list of general reference books and journals will give you some starting points for collecting bib and note cards. Keep looking for references that apply particularly to your group. For example, any study of schools or students might begin with the *Encyclopaedia of Educational Research* and the *Education Index.*

Reference Works

The American Behavioral Scientist. *The ABS Guide to Recent Publications in the Social and Behavioral Sciences.* New York: Sage Publications, 1965. (Supplements: 1966, 67, 68.)

Archer, M. S. *Current Research in Sociology: Published on the Occasion of the 8th World Congress of Sociology.* Atlantic Highlands, N.J.: Humanities Press, 1975.

Book Review Digest. New York: Wilson, 1905-date.

Clarke, Jack A., ed. *Research Materials in the Social Sciences.* 2nd ed. Madison: University of Wisconsin Press, 1967.

Education Index. New York: Wilson, 1929-date.

Gendell, Murray and Hans L. Zetterberg, eds. *A Sociological Almanac for the U.S.* New York: The Bedminister Press, 1961.

Harris, Chester W., ed. *Encyclopedia of Educational Research.* 3rd ed. New York: Macmillan, 1960.

Historical Statistics of the U.S., Colonial Times to 1957. Washington, D.C.: U.S. Bureau of the Census, 1960. Continuation to 1962 and Revision, 1965.

Hoselitz, Berthold F., ed. *A Reader's Guide to the Social Sciences.* Rev. ed. Glencoe: The Free Press, 1970.

International Bibliography of Sociology. Paris: UNESCO, 1952-date.

Lewis, Peter R. *The Literature of the Social Sciences: An Introductory Survey and Guide.* London: Library Association, 1960.

The New York Times Index, 1913-date.

Readers' Guide to Periodical Literature. New York: Wilson, 1900-date.

Social Sciences and Humanities Index. New York: Wilson, 1966-date. (Formerly *International Index to Periodicals,* 1907-1965.)

Sociological Abstracts. New York, 1952-date.

Statistical Abstract of the U.S. Washington, D.C.: U.S. Bureau of the Census, 1878-date.

Welsch, Erwin K. *The Negro in the U.S.: A Research Guide.* Bloomington: Indiana University Press, 1965.

White, Carl M. and associates. *Sources of Information in the Social Sciences: A Guide to the Literature.* Totowa: Bedminister Press, 1964.

Journals

Acta Socioligica
Adolescence
American Catholic Sociological Review
American Journal of Sociology
American Sociological Review
Annals of the American Academy of
  Political and Social Science
Australian and New Zealand Journal
  of Sociology
British Journal of Sociology
Crime and Delinquency
Harvard Educational Review
Human Organization

Human Relations
Indian Journal of Social Research
International Journal of Group Tensions
International Social Science Journal
Japanese Sociological Review
Journal of Marriage and the Family
Journal of Personality and Social Psychology
Journal of Political and Military Sociology
Journal of Social Issues
*Merrill-Palmer Quarterly of Behavior
    and Development*
Pacific Sociological Review
Public Opinion Quarterly
Rural Sociology
Sex Roles
Social Forces
Social Problems
Sociological Inquiry
Sociology of Education
Sociology and Social Research
Southwestern Social Science Quarterly
Teaching Sociology

Constructing

a

Questionnaire

Appendix C

Gathering clear data implies that you know what you're after and that formulating questions is a simple mechanical process. But in weighing the type, order, and wording of the questionnaire items, you will ask yourself again and again, "Just what do I expect to learn? What *am* I asking for?" This uncertainty is part of composition and a healthy sign that the reader will also find your work worth considering. In Chapter Five (Collecting the Data) we discussed some influences on composing questions, especially noting the direction given by your thesis; throughout this manual we have emphasized that a focused thesis and specific hypotheses make a penetrating term paper.

Questionnaire

The first requirement of your questionnaire is to develop information on the essential variables of your thesis. Questions about the religious zeal of college students, for example, should bring out this information:

1. Students' attitude about their zeal. Whether they think it has increased or decreased. What they think the influence of college has been.

2. Their behavior (to be measured against your idea of zeal). Whether they go to church more or less; defend their faith to skeptics; support personally and financially religious activities.

3. The reactions of family and friends. Whether members of the family think his or her zeal has changed. Whether friends have noticed a difference since the beginning of college.

Ideally the study would contact everyone involved, from parents and students to clerics and counselors. But the limits of a term paper will narrow the scope of inquiry, perhaps covering only the students' attitudes and perceptions.

Likewise, a survey exploring the extent of discrimination on a campus might touch several groups: teachers, administrators, secretaries, undergraduates, graduate students, dormitory residents, fraternity members, athletes. Sampling the several groups is one angle on narrowing the scope. The complementary angle is to sample the extent of discrimination of each person polled by asking key questions. The questions would explore these areas:

1. The respondent's biases, especially toward a particular group.

2. The respondent's idea of the existence or absence of bias, especially in work, in the classroom, on a team, or at a party. (For example, a woman may say that the school newspaper lets only men cover sports. A Jew may discuss his experience with fraternity exclusions. A black athlete may accuse a coach of using black players to warm the bench. And even an assistant professor may complain of being barred from voting in the election of department chairperson.)

The topic is clearly too broad; a questionnaire will uncover information too diffuse for a specific analysis of campus bias. We must reduce the number of groups sampled or the number of persons contacted or the number of variables considered—or all three. The first move is to identify the dependent variables (e.g., aspects of discrimination), then the independent variables, the factors you suspect cause or directly influence the dependent variables. Some independent variables in discrimination might be education, past associations with the discriminated or the discriminators, emotional and occupational security. Variables like age or sex, not causes but related closely to changes in the dependent variable, may be considered independent. Of course age or sex may sometimes directly cause variation: a boss may prefer to hire young, female secretaries, and a young female secretary may be rejected by older, female employees. Usually, however, the effect of age or sex on the dependent variable results from other factors revealed in further investigation. One way of inferring a more reasonable cause beneath age or sex or a similar variable is to *control* that variable. Appendix E gives an example. (Remember the earlier discussion of variables in Chapter Six.)

The possibility of such analyses depends on the kinds and number of questions in the survey. Factual questions you think might be worthwhile associating with one another or with questions on attitude are easy to ask and easy to answer. Being easy, they make a good start for a questionnaire by enabling the respondent to "succeed" immediately; they thus encourage the tackling of more difficult queries. But limit the factual beginning to four or five items. Otherwise a rapid fire of "age?" "sex?" "occupation?" "major?" "class?" makes the respondent feel like computer fodder. If more than four or five are necessary to your study, scatter them through the rest of the questionnaire as relief from the more challenging items.

After the first factual questions, introduce one or two questions to arouse the respondents' interest. Let them see that their opinions are necessary to you. For example, a survey of cocktail waitresses might include these questions as part of the beginning:

4. Do you have a favorite type of customer or not?
   _____yes
   _____no
   If "yes," what makes this type your favorite?

5. Is there a type of customer you dislike most or not?
   _____yes
   _____no
   If "yes," what makes this type so unlovable?

Questionnaire

The factual questions need your consideration too. Time employed, hours of shift, and previous employment might be good starters for interviews with waitresses. But questions on age, income, marital status, and education should be carefully worded and carefully placed. A pretest using two or three versions of your questionnaire would be good to see if your assumptions about sensitive questions and the resulting answers are sound. If you were interviewing, you could vary the approach to the central questions and see the reactions of the waitresses.

If you think a fact may be a sensitive point with a group, word the question to minimize annoyance or embarrassment. The relation of physical fitness to everyday demands of a job might make weight important for your hypothesis and unsettling for the respondents. Suppose you assumed that the weight requirement for police applicants derives from a belief that the emergencies of patrol duty call for officers in good physical shape. The measure of that shape might be a ratio of height and weight, so your interview schedule or questionnaire would have questions on both. Suspecting that the one on weight might inhibit overweight officers, you might consider options:

A. Weight:
_____ under 140
_____ 140-159
_____ 160-179
_____ 180-199
_____ 200 and over

B. Weight:
_____ 170 and under
_____ over 170

C. Weight:
_____ 169 or lighter
_____ 170 or heavier

D. Weight: _____

Of course option D should be most precise, but it may encourage white lies. Option A implies that the researcher expects certain weights to be significant. Options B and C show 170 as a crucial divide; option C is the touchy one, as "heavier" suggests "heavyset" and "overweight." (For further pointers on handling such questions, see Allen Barton's article on "Asking the Embarrassing Question," cited at the end of this appendix.)

A question may influence the respondent by its structure or wording. Such *bias* or *loading* can be subtle, but some basic precautions can be taken. Simple yes-no questions should provide both alternatives, and you should consider adding a neutral "don't know" or "undecided." Compare the following wordings:

A. Did you find the supplementary text helpful? _____

B. Did you find the supplementary text helpful? ____yes ____no

C. Did you find the supplementary text helpful? ____yes ____no

_____undecided

Faced with only the one blank of A, students of natural goodwill might say yes because supplementary texts are supposed to be helpful or because the friendly instructor was trying to help—or because the positive connotations of "helpful" suggest a positive response. But the "____no" of B directly challenges respondents' vague positive biases and reminds them to think through their own experiences. C gets fence-straddlers if you want them.

Multiple choice questions also must provide the option that might otherwise go unrecorded. Note that the second option in the following example uses a yes-no "filter question."

A. Major _____

B. Have you decided on a college major?

____yes (What is it? _____)
____no (What majors are you considering, if any? _____)

Here is another way of handling the same problem:

10. How often have you been drunk?

__a. once or twice __b. a few times __c. many times __d. never

The question is loaded because it assumes everyone has been drunk, but the final option withdraws the charge.

The loading often rests on a key word or phrase, as in the case of "170 or heavier" and "helpful." A neutral wording—or at least wording with balanced connotations—is most prudent in avoiding bias. The last sample question could replace the loaded "drunk" with the soberer "intoxicated" or "had too much to drink." Balancing

Questionnaire

connotations means making the possible answers sound equally acceptable:

21. How would you rate the instructor for helpfulness? (check one)
Very helpful   Helpful   Could be more helpful   Not very helpful
_____   _____   _____   _____

Sometimes balancing negative and positive connotations yields more valid information.

22. How would you rate the instructor's lectures? (check one)

Interesting	Somewhat Interesting	Seldom Interesting	Never Interesting
_____	_____	_____	_____

Not all loading should be avoided, however. Sometimes it can be especially useful when you think respondents would otherwise hesitate to give true answers. In Chapter Five we discussed using this technique to encourage students to be frank about cheating. Questions to encourage people to admit prejudice might need similar loading; neutral questions can mean neutral, safe answers. "Do you believe that blacks should have fewer rights than whites?" would probably bring a yes only from an extremist. A little suggestion might tap potential prejudice: "Are blacks now getting more 'equal rights' than the ordinary white citizen?" Attitudes, expecially unpopular ones, are hard to measure accurately because of their complexity. They are abstractions from a myriad of specific experiences and tend to reveal a different aspect for each specific application.

One structural method for getting reliable measures of an attitude is to space several questions to tap the same attitude. For example, a survey to determine racial bias in hiring might include the following questions. (Note that the numbers indicate spacing of the questions.)

8. Assuming that two applicants have equivalent academic and work backgrounds, which of these factors would influence you most in hiring?

_____a. dress _____b. social background _____c. religion _____d. race

_____e. physical appearance _____f. other (please specify) _____

[This last choice allows the respondent to explain or object.]

Questionnaire

15. If an employment agency wanted to send you someone, is there anything you would specify beyond the ability to do the job?

_____yes (What? _____)

_____no

_____don't know

21. Please rank the following qualities from 1 to 8 in order of importance for succeeding in business today. (1 is most important, 8 is least important.)

_____ Family background   _____ Race

_____ Schooling   _____ Work experience

_____ National origin   _____ Sex

_____ Religion   _____ Appearance

In question 29 (next page), adding questions on women relieves the employer who feels backed into the corner of racial discrimination. A rating scale like this one allows a crude scoring of respondents if you give a value to each point on the scale. Statements a, b, and g show bias if checked "strongly agree" or "agree." The wording of the other four statements reverses the pattern—"disagree" and "strongly disagree" reveal bias. (This reversal reduces the "halo effect," which comes from checking down a column without much thought, or from following an instantly recognized pattern of response.) Valid attitude scales are hard to construct, even for a professional. But you can make a valid attempt by thinking through your hypothesis again and by checking a reference like Allen Edwards' *Techniques of Attitude Scale Construction,* cited at the end of this appendix.

Those questions on discrimination show some of the variety possible in structured questions as well as a variety of attempts to get to the same point. The organization of the whole questionnaire moves the reader from routine factual information (kind of business, number of employees, location) to more and more complicated problems. The questions around number 8 would be multiple choice, and those

29. For each of the following statements please check the column that most closely approximates your belief.

	strongly agree	agree	uncertain	disagree	strongly disagree
a. An employer hesitates to hire a married woman because she probably will need time off to have a baby.					
b. An employer should provide black employees with extra supervision to ensure their efficiency.					
c. Even if a woman's salary supplements her husband's income, she should get the same salary as a married man doing the same job.					
d. References given by a black applicant are generally as reliable as those given by white applicants.					
e. A woman employee tends to bring out the best in her male co-workers.					
f. A black with an educacation equal to a white applicant probably had to work harder for it.					
g. An employer must serve the preference of the customers for white employees.					

Questionnaire

101

around number 15 would be a combination of structured and open-ended types. Rankings, ratings, and purely open-ended questions should go near the end of the questionnaire. (An alternative theory would put the questions asked specifically of the respondent in his business—numbers 8 and 15—after the general attitude survey of numbers 21 and 29.) But don't end with a battery of open-ended questions. The respondent, faced with the threat of several writing assignments, may simply give up and throw away your questionnaire.

As a relief from the challenges of this appendix, we will end with some basic points. Word your questions in language your reader understands. If technical language is unfamiliar and confusing the answers will be worthless. (And beware the tendency we all have of inflating our language when writing in public.) Limit the length of questions to about twenty words, and be sure that you and the respondent agree on the meaning of common but crucial terms. A very real semantic problem exists if you think "frequently" means once a week and the respondent thinks it means once a day. Even an everyday word like "study" has an amazing variation from student to student, as well as from student to instructor. Remember that you will have to tabulate and analyze the responses, so arrange the wording and layout of the questions to aid those tasks (see Appendix E).

If you would like more detail on questionnaires and interviews than we provide in this appendix and Chapter Five, try these sources:

Interviews, Observations and Questionnaires

Babbie, Earl R. *The Practice of Social Research*. Belmont: Wadsworth Publishing Company, Inc. 1975.

——. *Survey Research Methods*. Belmont: Wadsworth Publishing Company, Inc., 1973.

Barton, Allen. "Asking the Embarrassing Question," *Public Opinion Quarterly,* Vol. 22 (1958), pp. 67-68.

Blalock, Hubert M., Jr. *An Introduction to Social Research*. Englewood Cliffs: Prentice-Hall, Inc., 1970.

Bruyn, Severyn. *The Human Perspective in Sociology: The Methodology of Participant Observation*. Englewood Cliffs: Prentice-Hall, Inc., 1966.

Cole, Stephen. *The Sociological Method*. Chicago: Rand, 1972.

Edwards, Allen. *Techniques of Attitude Scale Construction*. New York: Appleton-Century-Crofts, 1957.

Forcese, Dennis and Stephen Richer. *Social Research Methods*. Englewood Cliffs: Prentice-Hall, Inc., 1973.

Gallup, George, Sr. "The Quintamensional Plan of Question Design," *Public Opinion Quarterly,* Vol. 11 (1947), pp. 385-393.

Gorden, Raymond. *Interviewing: Strategy, Techniques, and Tactics*. Homewood: Dorsey Press, 1975.

Hyman, Herbert H. *Survey Design and Analysis*. Glencoe: The Free Press, 1955.

____ and others. *Interviewing in Social Research*. Chicago: University of Chicago Press, 1975.

Kerlinger, Fred. *Foundations of Behavioral Research*. 2nd ed. New York: Holt, Rinehart and Winston, Inc., 1973.

McCall, George and J. L. Simmons. *Issues in Participant Observation*. Reading: Addison-Wesley Publishing Co., 1969.

Oppenheim, A. N. *Questionnaire Design and Attitude Measurement*. New York: Basic Books, 1966.

Riley, Matilda. *Sociological Research: Vol. I, A Case Study Approach*. New York: Harcourt, Brace and World, Inc., 1963.

Selltiz, Claire and others. *Research Methods in Social Relations*. Revised ed. New York: Holt, Rinehart and Winston, 1959.

Webb, Eugene J. and others. *Unobtrusive Measures: Nonreactive Research in the Social Sciences*. Chicago: Rand McNally and Co., 1966.

How to Read

to Read

a Table

Appendix D

WARRIORS	M	FG/A	FT/A	R	A	PF	PTS
Barry	43	15-28	7-7	6	8	2	37
Wilkes	28	7-13	1-2	7	1	3	15
Ray	24	1-5	1-3	11	1	4	3
C. Johnson	12	1-3	0-0	1	0	1	2
Smith	46	9-24	6-6	5	2	4	24
Williams	17	3-9	0-2	1	1	2	6
G. Johnson	24	7-8	1-2	10	1	2	15
Dickey	7	1-3	0-0	2	1	0	2
Dudley	21	1-2	0-0	4	6	2	2
Davis	18	3-6	4-4	6	0	4	10
TOTALS		48-101	20-26	53	21	24	116

KANSAS CITY	M	FG/A	FT/A	R	A	PF	PTS
Wedman	41	6-11	6-6	8	6	2	18
McNeill	22	2-6	0-2	5	0	5	4
Lacey	44	8-18	4-6	10	7	0	20
Archibald	45	10-15	7-9	3	8	3	27
Walker	36	10-18	3-4	3	3	3	23
Hansen	15	0-3	0-0	0	0	2	0
O. Johnson	11	2-4	0-0	2	0	0	4
Robertson	4	1-1	0-0	0	0	0	2
Robinzine	22	2-8	1-3	11	1	5	5
TOTALS		41-84	21-30	42	25	20	103

WARRIORS	24	31	23	38 — 116
KANSAS CITY	26	28	20	29 — 103

Shooting percentages: War. 47.5, KC 48.8
Blocked shots: Ray, G. Johnson, Davis, Archibald, Lacey 2, Wedman 2.
Officials: Strom, Saar
Turnovers: War. 15, KC 21.
Attendance: 7129.

		Sales			Net
Stocks Div	PE	Hds	Hi	Lo	Last Ch
BulovaW.20	200	$7^{7}/_{8}$	$7^{3}/_{8}$		$7^{5}/_{8}+$ $^{1}/_{2}$
BunkHill1.86	23	21	$20^{3}/_{4}$		$20^{3}/_{4}$
BunkRamo	68	$5^{1}/_{4}$	$5^{1}/_{8}$		$5^{1}/_{4}+$ $^{1}/_{4}$
Bunkrpfl1.50	17	$13^{5}/_{8}$	$13^{1}/_{2}$		$13^{5}/_{8}+$ $^{1}/_{8}$
Burlindl1.20	22 907	$31^{5}/_{8}$	$31^{1}/_{8}$		$31^{3}/_{8}-$ $^{1}/_{8}$
BurlNorth	13 234	$37^{1}/_{4}$	36		$36^{1}/_{8}-$ $^{3}/_{4}$
BurlNopf.55	16	$7^{1}/_{8}$	$6^{7}/_{8}$		$6^{7}/_{8}-$ $^{1}/_{8}$
Burndy.88	14 8	$39^{1}/_{2}$	$39^{3}/_{8}$		$39^{1}/_{2}+$ $^{1}/_{2}$
Burrghs.60	25 915	$102^{1}/_{8}$	100		$102^{1}/_{8}+1^{1}/_{8}$

San Francisco Chronicle, January 21, 1976, pp. 52 and 61 respectively.

Reading Tables

Every day millions of readers eagerly consume the information in these tables; but unless you follow basketball or the stock market, these neat columns and rows are as meaningless as a bingo card.

To understand a mystifying table, first try to relate it to your own interest. Find out what's in it for you. The second step is to examine the context of the table. Because statistical tables are an abstract, numerical language, they need a prose link to the concrete realities they represent. The strongest link is, of course, the chapter or article or term paper which includes the tables. But the titles, headings, and footnotes with the tables give the reader enough context to quickly assess his or her interest in the information. When constructing tables, be sure to provide such a brief context; and when reading tables, check the brief context before studying the numbers.

Begin examining a table by taking at least five seconds to ask yourself what numbers you think would fit the context of title, headings, and footnotes. This guessing clarifies your assumptions so that any difference between them and the researcher's information will be unmistakable. Ask yourself how the table could apply to your interest (your topic). Consider the limits of the information and the credibility of the source. Are facts on sorority girls at a certain campus valid for ''sorority girls''? For ''college students''? Is a survey showing the pills doctors take sponsored by a drug manufacturer of the most popular pill?

Consider this title: ''Enrollments for Appleby University, by Sex,[1] College, and Class: 1939 to 1974.'' If your topic were the influence on colleges of students with war experience, what questions might apply to this table?

1. Appleby U? Never heard of it. Must be small. A few vets might make a big impression at a campus of only a few hundred or a couple of thousand.

2. Is the time right? '39 to '74 includes World War II, the Korean War, the Vietnamese War. Should be a drop in male enrollment from '42 to '45, then a big increase—maybe even more than '39. Same around '52, and through the sixties.

3. Why the footnote at Sex? Aha, it was a girls' school until 1948, coeducational thereafter. Maybe they were taking advantage of G.I. Bill money or opening their doors to accommodate the demand.

4. By college? Must be big enough to allow several majors. Maybe things like Business Administration and Engineering will appear after '48. That would be a significant influence.

5. Private or public? Sectarian? A black college? Better check further before applying the information to "colleges."

6. Is the biggest college Literature and Arts—is it a liberal arts school? Is the biggest graduate school Education? Business? Did the vets enable them to start a graduate division? Maybe check out financing of the place to see if the government started any grants to encourage the admitting of vets.

7. Do the enrollments fluctuate according to the patterns of other colleges I've studied? Even though its enrollment may have increased after each war, it may have increased in a different proportion than other places experiencing the flood of vets.

If you had asked only one or two of these questions, your interest and understanding of the figures would be greater than had you obeyed the instinct to stare directly at the numbers until they made sense of themselves. They need help, and the table maker provides it with the context. But you can't expect the table or the tabulator to do everything. Use your eyes and use your head. Perhaps you can teach the tabulator something about his or her own information.

Here is a brief sample table abstracted from a widely read source of statistics:

No. 617. MEDIAN INCOME IN CONSTANT (1973) DOLLARS OF FAMILIES AND INDIVIDUALS, BY RACE: 1947 TO 1973

[Prior to 1960, excludes Alaska and Hawaii. See headnote, table 614]

YEAR	WHITE		NEGRO AND OTHER RACES		NEGRO AND OTHER RACES COMPARED WITH WHITE			
					Ratio[1]		Absolute difference in medians	
	Families	Unrelated individuals	Families	Unrelated individuals	Families	Unrelated individuals	Families	Unrelated individuals
1947	$ 6,285	$2,061	$3,212	$1,484	0.51	0.72	−$3,073	−$577
1950	6,405	2,058	3,449	1,509	0.54	0.73	− 2,956	−549
1955	7,673	2,326	4,236	1,575	0.55	0.68	− 3,437	−751
1960	8,758	2,791	4,848	1,602	0.55	0.57	− 3,910	−1,189
1965	10,210	3,161	5,677	2,339	0.56	0.74	− 4,533	−822
1970[2] ...	11,671	3,754	7,454	2,575	0.64	0.69	− 4,217	−1,179
1972[2] ...	12,193	3,915	7,534	2,905	0.62	0.74	− 4,659	−1,010
1973[2] ...	12,595	4,270	7,596	3,191	0.60	0.75	− 4,999	−1,079

[1] Ratios may differ from those calculated from current dollar distributions because of interpolation differences introduced in the derivation of constant dollar distributions.   [2] See footnote 1, table 614.

Source: United States Bureau of the Census, *Current Population Reports,* series P-60.

Copied from *Statistical Abstracts of the United States: 1974.* U.S. Bureau of the Census (Washington, D.C., 1974), p. 383.

"Median," not mean or mode. Why that measure? Maybe the mean would distort the information. How? So many of the very large incomes being nonwhite? (If "mean," "median," and "mode" mystify you, check Chapter Six again.) "Constant (1973) dollar"? Maybe it means the obvious—1973 buying power of the dollar used as a base to adjust the figures for other years. Better check. At the beginning of the section on "Income, Expenditures, and Wealth," a definition for "current and constant dollars" states that "data shown in constant dollars are computed values which eliminate the effect of price changes." What about terms like "families," "unrelated individuals," and "ratio"? Footnote at ratio. Better check it.

According to Table 617, unrelated individuals of "Negro and other races" do better in comparison with whites than do families of these nonwhites. The ratio between family incomes moved up nine percent from 1947 to 1973, with 1970 being the year nonwhite families came closest to the incomes of white families. The change has been irregular for unrelated individuals, with 1965 and 1972 being the years nonwhites in this category came closest to whites. Why a steady rise in the ratio for nonwhite family income and the relative steadiness of the ratio for nonwhite individuals? Why, too, that in 1973 the absolute difference in medians was greatest for families, but the greatest ratio difference is 1970?

In 1973, incomes of unrelated individuals are about a third of family incomes for whites; the incomes for unrelated nonwhites are about forty percent of the family incomes. Why the difference? What caused the family income of nonwhites to lose ground against white income in 1972 and 1973? What income did the government define as "poverty level" for those years? How did the addition of Alaska and Hawaii in 1960 affect the table? How would the addition of income from expense accounts, company cars, and phony income tax deductions make the figures look? Would whites and nonwhites have these in equal measure?

What about the influence of working women on family incomes? Maybe that's on the rise, which might account for the general rise in incomes. How much do nonwhite women contribute to family income as compared with white women? Try another set of data, Table 629. Would the figures be markedly different if done by race of wife? The averages here are means, and the income must be in current dollars, as the 1972 income of black women is $4,014—much higher than the $2,905 Table 617 reports for even "unrelated" nonwhites.

No. 629. WIFE'S CONTRIBUTION TO FAMILY INCOME— FAMILIES WITH HUSBAND AND WIFE WORKING, BY RACE OF HUSBAND: 1959 AND 1972

[Workers as of April 1960, and March 1973. See headnote, table 614. For States in each region, see fig. 1, inside front cover]

RACE, REGION AND CURRENT OCCUPATION GROUP OF WIFE	1959				1972			
	Husband-wife families, both working (1,000)	Average (mean) family income	Earnings of wife		Husband-wife families, both working (1,000)	Average (mean) family income	Earnings of wife	
			Average (mean)	Percent of family income			Average (mean)	Percent of family income
All white workers	12,282	$7,814	$2,097	26.8	19,103	$15,432	$3,932	25.5
North and West	9,040	8,112	2,144	26.4	13,068	15,986	4,023	25.2
South	3,242	6,986	1,967	28.2	6,035	14,231	3,737	26.3
White collar workers[1] .	5,420	9,064	2,819	31.1	10,003	17,488	5,059	28.9
North and West	3,950	9,314	2,878	30.8	6,849	18,023	5,163	28.6
South	1,470	8,392	2,682	32.0	3,154	16,327	4,832	29.6
All Negro workers	1,273	4,769	1,323	27.7	1,817	12,387	4,014	32.4
North and West	514	6,237	1,804	28.9	865	14,052	4,723	33.6
South	759	3,776	998	26.4	952	10,872	3,370	31.0
White collar workers[1] .	167	7,397	2,879	38.9	626	15,329	5,956	38.9
North and West	91	7,557	2,692	35.6	368	15,557	6,032	38.8
South	76	7,206	3,104	43.1	258	15,004	5,848	39.0

[1] Includes professional, managerial, clerical, and sales workers.

Source of tables 628 and 629: U.S. Bureau of the Census, *Current Population Reports*, series P-23, No. 39 and series P-60, No. 90.

Copied from *Statistical Abstracts of the United States: 1974,* U.S. Bureau of the Census (Washington, D.C., 1974), p. 388.

Figures are for whites and "Negroes," not "all other races." Percentages of white and black contributions of wives are pretty close. But in 1972 black wives contributed nearly five percent more than they did in 1959, and the contribution of white wives dropped about one percent. Why? Maybe black women were able to get jobs in other categories than "menial."

By asking questions like these, you can use a relevant table to give your study direction and depth. The figures no doubt will reflect a research approach different from yours, so remember that your data may differ from that shown in tables from *Statistical Abstracts*. At the very least, such tables provide interesting background for categories like "families," "race," and "income."

Some tables look confusing because they put a lot of information in front of you in a small space. Actually they are a blend of tables and can be read easily if you approach them calmly. Examine one part of the table at a time. Select data you need; don't summarize every fact given. Table 605 from *Statistical Abstracts* might be useful if you were curious about what percent or what amount of income spent on alcoholic beverages might define "excessive drinker."

After reading the title, headnote, and footnotes to check out any limitations that might be relevant to your study, examine the body of the table. Clearly the immediately valuable section in this one is the first, the list from "Food" to "Tobacco." Immediately this large table becomes a relatively small one, so you concentrate on understanding this part of Table 605.

Within that section is just the category you want: alcoholic beverages, which you see shows 7.9 for 1950, 9.1 for 1955, and so on at five-year jumps through 1965, when it goes 1965 to 1968, with yearly intervals through 1972. That last year the figure for alcoholic beverages is 20.3. That's quite a jump itself, 7.9 to 20.3.

What do those figures refer to? The headnote said "in billions of dollars, except percent." And with no mention of "constant dollars," you already know (from Table 617 and the introduction to this chapter on income, expenditures, and wealth) that unless specified "constant," the dollars are "current"—so the buying power of dollars may differ from year to year. Studying the data again, you can see that "total consumption" and "percent" appear in boldface type. The string of 100s following "percent" indicates that the figures above them must add up to 100, and are therefore percents. "Total consumption" must therefore be in billions of current dollars.

Now you know that in 1950 alcoholic beverages accounted for 7.9 percent of $191 billion. In 1972 they accounted for 20.3 percent of $726.5. So what?

The percent of expenditure on alcohol would probably be most relevant to a study you were doing on excessive drinking. (You would no doubt be finding out how much drinkers spent on alcoholic beverages per day or week or month, then working this into a percent of the drinkers' incomes to find some pattern of distribution that would indicate the group to be defined as excessive.) But, lo and behold, the small table of percents within Table 605 lumps alcoholic beverages in with food and tobacco, so it's back to the little table at the top.

Alcoholic beverages appears in two categories—"food" and "alcoholic beverages," so the first must mean that drinks bought as part of eating and drinking out are going to be hidden. You have to focus on beverages bought separately. Probably all right as excessive

No. 605. PERSONAL CONSUMPTION EXPENDITURES, BY PRODUCT: 1950 TO 1972

[In billions of dollars, except percent. Prior to 1960, excludes Alaska and Hawaii. Represents market value of goods and services purchased by individuals and nonprofit institutions, and value of food, clothing, housing, and financial services received by them as income in kind. Includes rental value of owner-occupied houses, but not purchases of dwellings. See also *Historical Statistics, Colonial Times to 1957*, series G 191-218]

TYPE OF PRODUCT	1950	1955	1960	1965	1968	1969	1970	1971	1972
Total consumption	191.0	254.4	325.2	432.8	536.2	579.5	617.6	667.2	726.5
Food, beverages[1], and tobacco .	58.1	72.2	87.5	107.2	125.1	130.7	141.2	148.3	157.9
Purchased meals, beverages[1] .	11.1	13.8	16.2	20.1	25.0	26.7	29.3	30.5	33.3
Food (excl. alcoholic beverages)...............	46.0	58.1	70.1	85.8	99.7	104.1	112.1	117.5	125.0
Alcoholic beverages	7.9	9.1	10.4	13.0	15.6	16.5	17.9	19.1	20.3
Tobacco	4.3	5.0	7.0	8.4	9.8	10.1	11.2	11.7	12.6
Clothing, accessories, and jewelry[2]..................	23.7	28.0	33.0	43.3	55.5	59.9	62.8	67.0	72.7
Woman's and children's[3]	10.0	12.4	14.8	19.7	25.3	27.3	29.0	31.7	34.5
Men's and boy's[3]	6.0	7.0	8.0	10.7	13.8	14.9	15.7	16.8	18.6
Jewelry and watches	1.3	1.7	2.1	2.9	3.8	4.1	4.3	4.3	4.6
Shoes, and shoe cleaning and repair	3.5	3.8	4.7	5.7	7.3	8.2	8.4	8.8	9.6
Personal care	2.4	3.5	5.3	7.6	9.0	9.8	10.4	10.6	11.1
Housing	21.3	33.7	46.2	63.5	77.3	84.1	90.9	98.5	105.5
Household operations[2]........	29.5	37.3	46.9	61.8	76.2	82.3	87.4	93.8	104.8
Furniture, equip., and supplies	16.6	19.5	22.8	30.8	38.9	42.2	44.3	47.3	53.3
Electricity	2.1	3.5	5.1	6.6	8.1	8.9	9.8	10.9	12.3
Gas	1.2	2.0	3.2	4.1	4.6	4.9	5.3	5.7	6.2
Telephone and telegraph	1.9	3.1	4.5	6.4	8.2	9.1	9.9	10.8	12.2
Domestic service	2.6	3.1	3.8	4.0	4.6	4.7	4.8	5.0	5.0
Medical care expenses	8.8	12.8	19.1	28.1	37.8	42.8	47.4	52.0	57.4
Personal business	6.9	10.0	15.0	21.9	29.5	33.3	35.3	38.6	41.2
Transportation	24.7	35.6	43.1	58.2	72.0	77.8	77.8	90.4	100.2
User-operated transportation..	21.9	32.6	39.8	54.4	67.3	72.6	72.3	84.6	93.9
Purchased transportation	2.8	3.0	3.3	3.8	4.7	5.1	5.5	5.8	6.2
Recreation	11.1	14.1	18.3	26.3	33.6	36.9	40.7	42.7	47.8
Private education and research ..	1.6	2.4	3.7	5.9	8.7	9.5	10.4	10.8	12.0
Religious and welfare activities .	2.3	3.3	4.7	6.0	7.6	8.1	8.6	9.1	10.1
Foreign travel and other, net ...	.6	1.6	2.2	3.2	3.8	4.2	4.8	5.2	5.7
Percent.................	100.0	100.0	100.0	100.0	100.0	100.0	100.0	100.0	100.0
Food, beverages[1], and tobacco .	30.4	28.4	26.9	24.8	23.3	22.6	22.9	22.2	21.7
Clothing, accessories, and jewelry	12.4	11.0	10.2	10.0	10.3	10.3	10.2	10.0	10.0
Personal care	1.3	1.4	1.6	1.8	1.7	1.7	1.7	1.6	1.5
Housing	11.1	13.3	14.2	14.7	14.4	14.5	14.7	14.8	14.5
Household operations	15.4	14.7	14.4	14.3	14.2	14.2	14.2	14.1	14.4
Medical care expenses	4.6	5.0	5.9	6.5	7.0	7.4	7.7	7.8	7.9
Personal business	3.6	3.9	4.6	5.1	5.5	5.7	5.7	5.8	5.7
Transportation	12.9	14.0	13.3	13.5	13.4	13.4	12.6	13.5	13.8
Recreation	5.8	5.5	5.6	6.1	6.3	6.4	6.6	6.4	6.6
Other	2.4	2.8	3.3	3.5	3.7	3.8	3.9	3.8	3.8

[1] Includes alcoholic beverages.　　[2] Includes items not shown separately.　　[3] Except footwear.

Source of table 604 and 605: U.S. Bureau of Economic Analysis; *The National Income and Product Accounts of the United States, 1929-1965; Survey of Current Business*, July issues; and unpublished data.

Copied from *Statistical Abstracts of the United States: 1974*, U.S. Bureau of the Census (Washington, D.C., 1974), p. 376.

Reading Tables

drinkers are going to buy a lot of alcohol to go. So the next step is to figure percents. Now you see that this small table is itself three tables: a general one listing food, beverages, and tobacco together; a small one listing purchased meals and beverages; and one that breaks the first into separate categories, with alcoholic beverages the middle one. So the expense for alcohol this table shows will be $7.9 \div 191.0 = 4.1$ percent for 1950. For 1972, it would be $20.3 \div 726.5 = 2.8$ percent. Now you can, for comparison, work your research so your data will include total expenses for each respondent. Then you could figure percent of total consumption for alcohol and compare directly with these figures. Or, to stick with percent of income spent on alcohol, you need to use a table of income along with Table 605.

Our interpretation of these tables comes from the brief context available in the *Statistical Abstract* and the numbers themselves. If a table appears as part of a researcher's study, the best way to discover the interpretation of the figures is to read the report—the full context. By becoming skilled in evaluating tables from the brief contexts, however, you can check the tables before reading the report. After checking them you may lose interest in the report because its coverage is too broad or too narrow for your topic. But if the tables look interesting, you will read the report with sharpened eyes.

Turning Data into Tables

Appendix E

Most of the tables you see in books and articles represent information selected from even more complicated preliminary tables. This simplification is normal because most researchers gather more information, or more specific information, than they decide is significant. For example, suppose the compilers of Table 605 (shown in Appendix D) had accumulated more detailed information on "medical care expense." That section of their original table might have looked like this for the section covering 1950:

TABLE 1

Personal Consumption Expenditures, by Product: 1950 to 1972

Medical care[1]	8.8
Hospitals	3.3
Doctors	2.8
Dentists	.9
Podiatrists, chiropractors	.5
Medical insurance premiums[2]	1.3

[1]All these expenses are out of pocket—after any bills have been paid by an insurance plan.

[2]Counts premiums paid as fringe benefits by employers.

The final table would, perhaps, have come from a decision to break down only categories relevant to industrial manufacturers.

In this example, statisticians might thus have "collapsed" detailed information into one category. Use this technique if you have more data for your report than is worth the reader's attention. You can minimize this step by being clear about just what information you need to test your hypotheses, which means, roughly, figuring out the shape of the tables as you make up your interview schedule or questionnaire.

If you have access to a computer or card-sorter, code your structured responses for card punching. You can save time, lots of it, by building some of the coding operations into your interview schedule or questionnaire. If you are less privileged (or less venturesome) and thus rely on handpower, planning your questionnaire for coding can save even more time. Hints for the machineless student are rare, but the following description should reduce this rarity by one or two persons.

On page 49 we suggested arranging the interview schedule (which you will fill out) with spaces for responses to "quantified" questions *vertically* at the left edge of your paper. For example:

_____yes, frequently   15. Are you ever depressed about your life?
_____yes, occasionally   (if yes) about how often?

_____no

_____no control   16. Now let's change the subject a bit. There's
_____some control   a lot of talk these days about how much
     fairly strong   freedom in sexual expression students
_____control   should have. Some people say that col-
                              leges should offer students firm guiding
_____strong control   controls, others say that students should
                              have no restrictions whatsoever. How
                              much control do you think colleges should
                              have over a student's sex life?

If you've asked a hundred persons twenty or twenty-five questions, your job is to move the answers from 100 separate sheets to one or more coherent tables. You might be interested in how males and females differ on a question, or on how marijuana users differ from nonusers. Construct tabulation sheets with your independent variables (sex, use of marijuana or whatever you choose) arranged horizontally, with a line between the categories:

Tab Sheet   Table 2
Marijuana Use

                          Depression by Marijuana Use
Depressed: *user*   *nonuser*
frequently
occasionally
never

	user	nonuser
frequently		
occasionally		
never		

Data into Tables

Table 3

College Control of Sex by
Marijuana Use

Control:	*user*	*nonuser*
none		
some		
fairly strong		
strong		

Make a rough draft of your tables next with this method:

1. Sort your questionnaires into two piles: ''marijuana users'' and ''non-users.'' (Of course, if your data allow you could have any number of piles: ''frequent use,'' ''occasional use,'' ''once or twice,'' ''non-use''—in which case, your tab sheet would have a corresponding number of columns.)

2. Take one pile (''users'') and lay it over the tab sheet, such that the corresponding category (''users'') on the tab sheet is next to the left edge of the pile.

3. Tally the responses in the appropriate boxes. (Our illustration shows the tallying of the thirty-sixth sheet.)

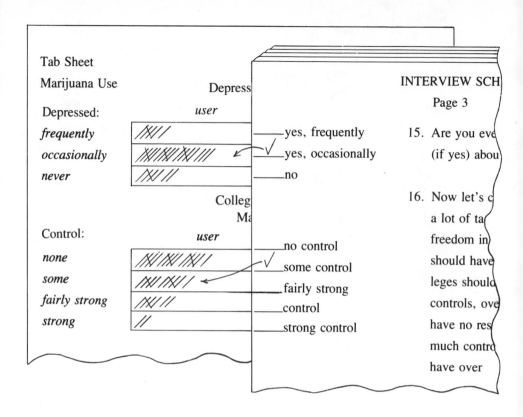

After all piles have been tallied, the resulting table (for 100 question-naires) needs only polish and interpretation:

Data into Tables

These illustrations show only two tables developed from one page of the questionnaire, but you could easily accommodate four, five or more tables on a single 8½ × 11 tally sheet. Your survey would still require a good number of pages, but in our current economy, paper usually is cheaper than time.

As suggested in Chapter Six (Analyzing the Data), you may want to observe the effects of a third variable on your original two. The hand-tabulating would be the same, but you would divide the questionnaires into more piles and use a more elaborate tab sheet:

Tab Sheet

Marijuana Use

and Sex

Table 4

Depression by Marijuana Use and Sex

	Males		Females	
Depressed:	*user*	*nonuser*	*user*	*nonuser*
frequently				
occasionally				
never				
Number				

Note again the importance of planning: you can derive two-variable tables from three-variable tables. If you recognize beforehand that the more complicated analysis is necessary, skip the first tabulation.

Select the tables that most effectively portray the significant findings and include each in the text near your explanation of the point it demonstrates. Always refer to the tables by number—and check the final draft of your paper to be sure that your explanations refer to the right tables. If the tables fit awkwardly into the text or if there are many, you may include them in an appendix at the end of the paper. But if your reader must study the tables to appreciate your point, place them in the text to make the job easier. And wherever you use them, provide a full definition of each of the variables and their sub-categories. Some of this information is carried in an adequate title, some of it in footnotes to the table, some in the context of the report. All of it should help your reader understand your tables and the adequacy of your interpretation.

Include at least one explanatory sentence in the text for each one of your tables. Don't leave it up to the reader to figure out the main point of a table. And stick to a conventional design for your tables as it makes reading them easy for your instructor. The one for a multivariable table has the independent variable across the top with the data for it in the columns; the dependent variable is along the left side with the data for it across the rows. Any additional independent or controlling variables go under the main independent variable. Therefore, in table 4 (Depression by Marijuana Use and Sex), "depression" is the dependent variable, and "marijuana use and sex" are the independent variables. The total of all the values in a single row or column is the *marginal* of that category. Each row and column, therefore, has its own marginal.

Percentaging is a basic method of comparing different parts of a table. It is possible to make a variety of comparisons with a table by percentaging different ways. (A simple hand-held calculator is a big help.) If you want to see the relation of one category of respondents to the whole sample, select the marginal of that category and divide it by the total number of respondents. Table 5 (Influence of Political Ideology upon Attitudes Toward the Legalization of Marijuana) shows that 52 percent of the respondents disagree with the legalization of marijuana. The percentage is a clearer statement of comparison than the raw data.

Table 5

Influence of Political Ideology upon
Attitudes Toward the Legalization of Marijuana

		Conservative	Liberal	
Attitudes	Agree	20	35	55
Toward	Disagree	32	28	60
Legalization		52	63	115

You can make another percentage description within any one row or column by dividing the cell value by the marginal total. For example, of the sixty respondents who disagree with the legalization of marijuana, 53 percent are conservative and 47 percent are liberal. If you wish to focus on one group, this percentage will help describe the distribution of the cross-tabulated variable for that group.

Because percentaging allows such clear comparison to discuss the results for a hypothesis, use it within each category of the independent variable. Then compare these percentages across any one category of the dependent variable. In Table 5 you would percentage within the "conservative" column $(20 \div 52)$ $(32 \div 52)$ and within the "liberal" column $(35 \div 63)$ $(28 \div 63)$. These results indicate that 18 percent more liberals than conservatives (56 percent to 38 percent) agree with legalization of marijuana. You might compare across the "disagree" category and conclude that 18 percent more conservatives than liberals disagree with the legalization (62 percent to 44 percent). (You could describe these results in a ratio statement by dividing the smaller value into the large one— $35 \div 20 = 1.75$. The conclusion would be that for every conservative who agrees with the legalization, there are 1.75 liberals who agree.)

A final note: Be sure to give each of your tables a number and title that identifies the dependent and independent variables. If you percentage the data in a table, be sure to indicate in parentheses the total number of respondents included in that table.

Chi-Square
and Other
Statistics

Appendix F

In Chapter Six (Analyzing the Information) we discussed briefly some essential statistics—raw numbers, percents, averages, and associations. This appendix extends that discussion slightly to encourage you to try methods commonly used by sociologists to describe and test results. If you've had a course in statistics, our elementary explanations will seem elementary indeed. Their point is to unpack the basic tools and demonstrate only a few of their uses. The books listed at the end of our discussion explore wider applications and even shortcuts to assembling these tools. (Though these statistical measures require no mathematics beyond arithmetic, the calculations, without some kind of calculator, can be tedious.) But remember that though numbers look impressively exact—especially next to decimal points—statistics are only as good as a sound sample and questionnaire.

Before using a particular measure, ask yourself if the values you intend to test are *continuous* or *noncontinuous*. Variables with values arranged along a scale without a break are continuous. Age, for example, is continuous, but race is not. Years of schooling is continuous, but areas of study are not. Anyone's age falls along a continuum with an infinite number of points between one end (zero) and the other (perhaps 120). Continuous data can be treated mathematically; for example, age 50 is twice age 25 and mid-way between 49 and 51. But there is no such continuum established for "white" and "black." These terms refer to society's definitions, which are not made with a light meter. Likewise, the relationship between "political science," "art," and "physics" cannot be added, subtracted or multiplied. But schooling progresses smoothly from first grade through college to graduate school, where the continuum becomes confusing. The grade designations from first through twelfth are continuous, and the measure of progress through college usually is the continuous accumulation of credits. But class designations such as freshman and sophomore, without reference to number of credits, are noncontinuous.

There are a number of ways the association between two variables can be stated mathematically. In Chapter Six and Appendix E we described some of the best and most basic—ratios, percentages, and averages. But simply choosing a technique you're familiar with and computing properly may very well lead to a false and misleading conclusion. A reference book on statistics can help you decide which associational technique is best for your data if this book doesn't seem to have an appropriate one. (See the end of this appendix for a list of such reference books.) If you have a problem applying statistics sometimes the most direct and efficient thing to do is ask someone who has had the necessary background. But remember, you don't have to use sophisticated statistical analysis to write an interesting, sociologically solid paper.

The *chi-square* test applies to relationships among variables of which at least one is noncontinuous. The chi-square test compares the relationship established by your findings with the relationship that would occur purely by chance. Looking at your research with a gambler's eye, you ask if the odds are good that the differences within your sample will apply to other samples that could be drawn in the same way from the same population. In other words, is it safe to bet that your sample differences represent differences in the whole population? Obviously the chi-square test applies to a group you study as a sample of a large group. And remember that it includes noncontinuous data.

Suppose your poll of a sample had included the following questions on stealing and on race to explore the moral fibre of your group.

   3. Which race are you usually considered part of?

      _____green _____red _____other

  12. Many people have occasionally yielded to impulse and taken something not belonging to them. Have you done so in the past year?

      _____yes _____no

    If yes, take a guess at how many dollars worth of stuff you've taken in the past year: _____

To see if there is any relationship between race and theft, first tabulate the information. If there is an interesting difference, apply the chi-square test.

TABLE 1

Race

		Green	Red	Other	Totals
Theft	yes	46	6	2	54
	no	29	11	1	41
	Totals	75	17	3	95

This table, drawn from answers to number 3 and the first part of number 12, shows the number of cases from the ninety-five returned questionnaires form a curious pattern. Note that both variables are noncontinuous, and also keep in mind that tables for chi-square calculation present raw numbers, *not* percents.

Statistics

A restriction of chi-square is that the "expected value" for each cell must be at least five. An expected value is the result of multiplying the row total and column total of a cell and dividing it by the total number of scores. Thus, the expected value for the Yes/Green cell is 75 × 54 ÷ 95 = 42.5 (rounded to 43). If an expected value is less than five, chi-square is not the appropriate tool. This expected value problem occurs most frequently when you have a small sample—less than thirty respondents. To solve the problem of small expected values in Table 1, we consolidated to create Table 2.

TABLE 2

Race

		Green	Non-green	Totals
	yes	46	8	54
Theft				
	no	29	12	41
	Totals	75	20	95

Setting aside the conclusions you might draw from this data and the percents you might calculate, let's plunge right into calculating the chi-square. Here is the formula:

$$x^2 = \sum \frac{(f_o - f_e)^2}{f_e}$$

x^2 = chi-square
$\sum$ = "the sum of"

f_o = "the observed frequency" (the number of cases in each cell of your table)

f_e = "the expected frequency" (the number of cases in each cell expected by pure chance)

Table 3 shows the expected frequencies in parentheses, which makes it a working table; the finished table in your report might include percents, but not expected frequencies.

TABLE 3

Race

		Green	Non-green	Totals	%
	yes	46 (43)	8 (11)	54	57
Theft					
	no	29 (32)	12 (9)	41	43
	Totals	75 (75)	20 (20)	95	100

Here is another simple way to determine the expected frequency of "Green thieves": (1) find what percent of the total sample answered "yes" (57%); (2) multiply that percent by the total of Green cases (.57 × 75 = 43). Do the same for each of the other cells (.57 × 20 = 11; .43 × 75 = 32; .34 × 20 = 9). The results show what would be expected if the proportion of thieves in both racial categories were the same. The calculation of the chi-square figure follows the formula:

$$\Sigma \; \frac{(fo - fe)^2}{fe}$$

$$\frac{(46 - 43)^2}{43} + \frac{(29 - 32)^2}{32} + \frac{(8 - 11)^2}{11} + \frac{(12 - 9)^2}{9} =$$

$$\frac{9}{43} + \frac{9}{32} + \frac{9}{11} + \frac{9}{9} =$$

$$.21 + .28 + .82 + 1 = 2.31$$

Before interpreting this chi-square figure, let's consider another table drawn from the answers to those two questions on thievery.

TABLE 4

Theft by Race

		Green	Red	Other	Totals
	Grand Thieves ($50+)	34	1	1	36
Persons	Petty Thieves ($1 - $49)	12	5	3	20
	Straights	29	11	1	41
	Totals	75	17	5	97

This time the table includes a continuous variable, value of stolen goods, and the noncontinuous variable of race. It contains nine cells, but again those under "Other" are less than five. Following the steps outlined before creates Table 5.

TABLE 5

Theft by Race

		Green	Non-green	Total	%
	Grand Theft ($50+)	34 (29)	2 (8)	36	37
Persons	Petty Thieves ($1 - $49)	12 (15)	8 (5)	20	21
	Straights	29 (32)	12 (9)	41	42
	Totals	75 (76)*	22(22)	97	100

*Difference due to rounding error.

Remember that for both the basic tables we want to know if the observed difference between the two racial categories in the proportion of thieves and kinds of thieves is an accident of the sample or if it exists in the total population. The next step, then, is to apply your chi-square figures to a table of probabilities to see what the odds are of picking up the differences by pure chance. Here is an excerpt from such a table:

TABLE 6

Probabilities Related to Chi-Square

Probabilities

No. of Cells	.30	.20	.10	.05	.02	.01	.001
2 × 2	1.07	1.64	2.71	3.84	5.41	6.64	10.83
2 × 3	2.41	3.22	4.60	5.99	7.82	9.21	13.82
2 × 4	3.66	4.64	6.25	7.82	9.84	11.34	16.27
3 × 3	4.88	5.99	7.78	9.49	11.67	13.28	18.46
3 × 4	7.23	8.56	10.64	12.59	15.03	16.81	22.46
4 × 4	10.66	12.24	14.68	16.92	19.68	21.67	27.88

The first chi-square figure (2.31) came from a 2 × 2 table (four cells), so it falls between the probabilities of .20 and .10. We could expect to match the findings of our sample by sheer accident with between twenty to ten percent of similar samples drawn from the population. In other words, the odds are between five to one and ten to one. Finding the exact probability is unnecessary; it is conventionally expressed as lying between probabilities: .20 ⟩ p ⟩ .10, with ''⟩'' meaning ''is greater than.'' The second chi-square figure, 7.00, falls between .05 and .02 in the row for 2 × 3 tables. The odds for a chance matching of that sample are between twenty to one and fifty to one (.05 ⟩ p ⟩ .02).

How much would you bet on your findings with odds like that?

Some researchers accept a finding if they can show that it could have developed by chance alone less than five times in a hundred, others accept only a "2% level of confidence" (two times out of a hundred) or a "1% level." Some, however, accept none at all, arguing that such a test is usually misleading. If you do use such a test, keep in mind that at best it is only an indication that *chance alone* does not explain the differences. But if not chance, what? Perhaps sample bias, perhaps interview bias, perhaps an error in addition. The list of possibilities could continue for some length before you reach the conclusion that most students jump to: perhaps the differences are indications of "real" differences.

Unless you are versed in the requirements, avoid using "tests of significance" or other statistical measures. Simply look at your data and tables with a critical eye, asking yourself the basic question only dimly represented in the chi-square: Are these relationships valid characterizations of my sample? And even if they are, do they deserve my attention?

Standard Deviation and Coefficient of Correlation

The standard deviation is central to a great many other statistical measures, but we will concentrate on its role in the calculation of correlation coefficients. Basically, standard deviation is a context for a mean, which is the arithmetic center of a distribution of values (see page 61). Because the mean says nothing about the range of values, it can sometimes distort the interpretation of them. Consider these distributions of (fictitious) scores in exams from two sections of the same sociology course:

Section A		Section B	
90-100	2	90-100	
80-89	4	80-89	
70-79	8	70-79	20
60-69	3	60-69	
50-59	3	50-59	
	20		20

$$\text{Mean}_A = \frac{(95 \times 2) + (85 \times 4) + (75 \times 8) + (65 \times 3) + (55 \times 3)}{20}$$

$$\text{Mean}_B = \frac{75 \times 20}{20}$$

$$M_A = 74.5 = 75 \qquad\qquad M_B = 75$$

Short of reproducing the exact distribution of scores (number of 71's, 68's, etc.) or these tables, what would picture the difference between these distributions? A simple statement could do it: "Scores in Section A range from 53 to 97; in Section B they range from 70 to 78." That would be fine for such a simple pair of distributions, but imagine the problem in trying to discover the spread of 200 scores from 0 to 100—and then trying to compare two such distributions. Some calculated measure must assist the eye.

If the group of scores is not meant as a sample, the *average deviation* (from the mean) will serve. That figure, with the mean and range, characterizes fairly a set of continuous data.

$$\text{average deviation} = \frac{\text{sum of deviations from the mean (all considered positive)}}{\text{total number of cases}}$$

For section A, the average deviation is:

$$\frac{(95 - 75)2 + (85 - 75)4 + (75 - 75)8 + (75 - 65)3 + (75 - 55)3}{20} = \frac{170}{20} = 8.5$$

For Section B it is: $\dfrac{(75 - 75)20}{20} = 0$. Simple.

As most sociological research considers a particular group as a sample of a population, the average deviation must some way respond to the greater range of values available in the totality. Logic (or common sense) suggests that the range of even the most carefully chosen sample will probably be less than the range of the whole population. If Section A of that sociology course samples all sections of that course ever taught, we wonder if one poor devil hadn't scored less than 50. And we would be fools to judge the history of that exam on the basis of Section B. How can the average deviation of a sample fit the whole population?

We first assume that whatever extremes appear in a sample will be exaggerated in the population. The *standard deviation* formalizes this exaggeration.

$$\text{standard deviation} = \sqrt{\frac{\text{total of } \textit{squared} \text{ deviations from the mean}}{\text{total number of cases}}}$$

Statistics

Squaring the deviations is an effort at imagining the potential range of cases. It may be mistaken, but it is a step better than blind faith. Let's see how it differs from the average deviation in describing the population sampled by the scores in Section A.

$$\sqrt{\frac{(95-75)^2\times 2 + (85-75)^2\times 4 + (75-75)^2\times 8 + (75-65)^2\times 3 + (75-55)^2\times 3}{20}} =$$

$$\sqrt{\frac{800 + 400 + 0 + 300 + 1200}{20}} = \sqrt{\frac{2700}{20}} = \sqrt{135} = 11.6$$

The standard deviation suggests a thirty-five percent rise in the average deviations from the mean over the whole population ($\frac{11.6-8.5}{8.5}$). Such a large increase might be expected from the small number of cases in the sample; but using the standard deviation, we can cautiously extend those few cases beyond our immediate view.

Standard deviation is necessary to the calculation of a *coefficient of correlation*, a single number that shows the relationship between two continuous variables. Instead of vaguely referring to "high" or "low" correlations, you use the coefficient to put the correlation on a continuum so its relation to other correlations is at once clear. Readers familiar with the coefficient values, which range from -1 (high negative) to $+1$ (high positive), can see at a glance how two variables relate. A correlation of zero means the two variables change completely independent of one another—a zero relationship.

Let's go back to the study that uncovered a gang of thieves in your sample. Suppose you had included a question to find out each respondent's highest completed grade in school, counting the first four years of college as grades thirteen through sixteen. To simplify our example, we are cutting down the study from ninety-five to ten because standard deviation requires the figuring of each case separately, and correlation requires the matching of two values for each case. Thus, though the process is simple, the mechanics take a couple of pages of figures (unless you care to learn a shortcut from one of the reference books).

Case	Thievery	Case	Education
1	$100	6	16
2	60	8	15
3	50	10	14
4	25	4	13
5	25	2	12
6	10	7	12
7	8	3	11
8	2	9	11
9	0	5	10
10	0	1	8
	$280		122 years

$$\text{Mean}_1 = \frac{280}{10} = \$28 \qquad \text{Mean}_2 = \frac{122}{10} = 12 \text{ years}$$

$$\text{S.D.}_1 = \sqrt{\frac{\begin{array}{l}(100-28)^2 + (60-28)^2 + (50-28)^2 + \\ 2(25-28)^2 + (10-28)^2 + (8-28)^2 + \\ (2-28)^2 + 2(0-28)^2\end{array}}{10}} = \sqrt{968} \quad \text{S.D.}_1 = 31$$

$$\text{S.D.}_2 = \sqrt{\frac{\begin{array}{l}(16-12)^2 + (15-12)^2 + (14-12)^2 + \\ (13-12)^2 + 2(12-12)^2 + 2(11-12)^2 \\ + (10-12)^2 + (8-12)^2\end{array}}{10}} = \sqrt{5} \quad \text{S.D.}_2 = 2.2$$

Given the means and the standard deviations, you can calculate the coefficient of correlation from the following formula.

$$\text{coefficient of correlation} = \frac{\Sigma xy}{N(\text{S.D.}_1)\,(\text{S.D.}_2)}$$

Σxy = the total of the multiplied deviations from the means of each case.

N = the number of cases.

Statistics

Match the figures of theft and education for each case, and you can figure the correlation coefficient.

Case	Thievery	Education
1	$100	8
2	60	12
3	50	11
4	25	13
5	25	10
6	10	16
7	8	12
8	2	15
9	0	11
10	0	14

$$\text{correlation} = \frac{\begin{array}{l}(72)(-4) + (32)(0) + (22)(-1) + (-3)(1) + \\ (-3)(-2) + (-18)(4) + (-20)(0) + (-26)(3) + \\ (-28)(-1) + (-28)(2)\end{array}}{10(31)(2.2)}$$

$$= \frac{(-519) + 34}{(31)(22)} = \frac{-485}{682} = -.71$$

This coefficient clearly shows a strong negative correlation between years of schooling and worth of goods stolen.

That figure of $-.71$ looks precise as well as high, but remember it comes from only ten cases. High correlations for large samples are indeed impressive, if the correlation isn't distorted. But note the influence of one case—number one, whose thievery is far above average and whose education is far below. This person accounts for -288 of the numerator. Eliminating that person from the sample (and thus using nine cases) reduces the correlation to $-.42$, which still shows a moderate relationship between education and theft. Of course, as we mentioned in Chapter Six (Analyzing the Data), correlation only marks a relationship (or lack of one). Two measures that covary are not necessarily related causally. If the figures on thievery and schooling were valid for the population, increasing schooling wouldn't necessarily mean reducing thievery. Perhaps persons disposed to thievery drop out, or perhaps better educated persons make more money and are less inclined to moonlight as thieves. A moderate or high correlation would call for deeper investigation.

A general caution: any sample with fewer than 100 cases is statistically weak (unless your population is about 200). But a sample of about 200 is surprisingly strong, even for a very large population— like 100,000—because probabilities change radically in the first cases but very little in subsequent ones. For example, the chance of flipping a coin twice and getting two heads in a row is $\frac{1}{4}$ (i.e., $\frac{1}{2} \times \frac{1}{2}$). The chance of flipping five in a row is $\frac{1}{32}$. But the odds are just over 1,000 to one against flipping ten heads in a row. The odds against flipping only ten times that number in a row (100) are 1,267,650,600,228, 229,401,496,703,205,376 to one. The chance of your drawing a sample of 200 or more for a term paper is small; but that only cautions you about generalizing from your limited data to a large population. It definitely does not mean you should assume a small study is worthless. On the contrary, thought provoking small studies often lead to significant large ones.

Statistics and Sampling

Alterman, Hyman. *Numbers at Work: The Story and Science of Statistics.* New York: Harcourt, Brace & World, Inc., 1966.

Blalock, Hubert, Jr. *Social Statistics.* 2nd ed. David M. Edwards, ed. New York: McGraw-Hill Book Company, Inc., 1972.

Champion, Dean. *Basic Statistics for Social Research.* Scranton: Chandler Publishing Company, 1970.

Downey, Kenneth. *Elementary Social Statistics.* New York: Random House, 1975.

Huff, Darrell. *How to Lie With Statistics.* New York: Norton, 1954.

Korin, Basil. *Statistical Concepts for the Social Sciences.* Cambridge: Winthrop Publishers, Inc., 1975.

Loether, Herman J. and Donald G. McTavish. *Descriptive Statistics for Sociologists.* Boston: Allyn and Bacon, Inc., 1974.

____. *Inferential Statistics for Sociologists.* Boston: Allyn and Bacon, Inc., 1974.

McCollough, Celeste and Loche Van Alta. *Introduction to Descriptive Statistics and Correlation: A Program for Self-Instruction.* New York: McGraw-Hill, 1965.

Mendenhall, William and others. *Statistics: A Tool for the Social Sciences.* North Scituate: Duxbury Press, 1974.

Runyon, Richard and Audrey Haber. *Fundamentals of Behavioral Statistics.* 3rd ed. Reading: Addison-Wesley Publishing Co., 1976.

Siegel, Sidney. *Nonparametric Statistics for the Behavioral Sciences.* New York: McGraw-Hill Book Company, Inc., 1956.

Slonim, Morris. *Sampling.* New York: Simon and Schuster, 1966 (originally titled *Sampling in a Nutshell,* 1960).

Stahl, Sidney M. and James D. Hennes. *Reading and Understanding Applied Statistics: A Self-Learning Approach.* St. Louis: C. V. Mosby Co., 1975.

Walpole, Ronald E. *Introduction to Statistics.* 2nd ed. New York: Macmillan Publishing Co., 1974.

Epilogue

When your term paper comes back with the instructor's approval, don't throw it away with the idea "another obstacle out of the way." It embodies a stage of your intellectual growth, and it no doubt has started you thinking over new ideas and asking new questions. Every rereading of the paper will bring back those ideas and questions, leading you to deepen your insights by exploring the topics further. It may become the basis for another paper—even, perhaps, for a dissertation.

We hope the paper leads you to continue to look more carefully, and more sociologically, at everyday life. The techniques and methods presented in this book are lenses that are always available to clarify and sharpen your interest in the world. As you look back on the interest that led to your topic, see how your impressions have changed or remained constant. Then think of another of your interests. How would you develop it through a research project? If we have been successful, this book will have helped make such a question interesting rather than intimidating.

Index

context, tables, 105-111, 118
continuous data, 121, 125, 128; *see also* variable
contractions, writing, 72
contrary hypothesis, 36
control, group, 57
control, variable, 57-59, 96
convenience, group selection, 36-38
correlation, *see* coefficient of correlation
current dollars, *see* dollars

deductive reasoning, thesis, 37
defining terms, 13-14, 21, 23, 71
dependent variable, 56; *see also* variable
depression, variable, 114-118
detail, writing, 68-70, 72-73
diet, topic, 38-39
discrimination on campus, topic, 95-96
doctors, *see* abortion
documentation, *see* footnote; further reference, 83-84; textual documentation
dollars, constant, 106-107, 109; current, 106-107, 109
doughnut deliveries, *see* honor system
drawing conclusions, 37, 62, 123; *see also* cause and effect
dress, topic, 3
drift of topic, 14
drinking, topic, student, 18-22, 56; tables, 109, 111

education, variable, *see* theft
Education Index, 30
Edward, Allen, 100
Encyclopaedia Britannica, 28
encyclopaedia, general, 28-29
Encyclopaedia of the Social Sciences, 29
Erikson, Kai T., 49
ethics, *see* research ethics

expected frequency, 123-126; *see also* observed frequency
explanation, variable, 58-59

fact, data as reality, 54, 59; documentation, 76, 91; note card, 32
families, *see* white race, black race, table
farming, topic, 5-6
filter question, 41, 98
fitness, *see* police fitness
football fans, topic, 88-91
footnote, 76-79; examples, 79; explanatory, 79; forms, 76-78; further reference, 83-84; Latin abbreviations, 76; tables, 105-110, 118; *see also* textual documentation
foreign students, topic, 11-12
formality, writing, 72
free question, *see* open question
frequency distribution, 60
further references, format, 83-84; general, 91-92; interview, 102-103; journals, 92-93; observation, 102-103; questionnaire, 102-103; sampling, 132-133; statistics, 132-133

Gallup, George, Sr., 41
gambling, *see* jockeys
GPA, *see* grade point average
grade point average, topic, 57-59
graphic aids, 69-70
green race, 122-125; *see also* race, red, theft
group, 2, 3, 19, 36-37, 57; control, 57; convenience, 36-38; heterogeneous, 51; homogeneous, 50-51; identification, 3; restriction, 14-15; sampling, 37-39; size, 37; subgroups, 50
group identification, topic, *see* dress

Hemingway, Ernest, 9, 64, 74
heroin use, topic, 54-55

heterogeneous group, 51
historical topics, 27
hockey fans, topic, 50-51
homogeneous group, 50-51
honor system, topic, 36-37
housing bias, topic, 64-68

"I", writing, 70-71
income, variable, census tables, 106-108; excessive drinking, 109-110; grade point average, 57-59
independent variable, 56; *see also* variable
index cards, 28, 30
indices, preliminary research, 28-32, 85, 87
individual, selecting a group, 3-4, 36-37; unrelated (census tables), 106-108
inductive reasoning, thesis, 37
informality, writing, 72
information question, *see* filter question
intensity question, 42-43
International Bibliography of Sociology
International Index, see *Social Sciences* and *Humanities Index*
interpretation, library research, 27; tables, 105-111; variable, 58-59
interview, 39, 45-49, 114-117; coding, 49, 113-117; embarrassing questions, 48; further reference, 102-103; notes, 47; open-ended, 45-46, 49; pretest, 46-49; probes, 46; interviewer's introduction, 45; schedule, 46-47, 114-117; tape recorder, 47
IQ, variable, 57-58; *see also* grade point average
irrelevant questions, 39
issues, topic, 4-6, 14
item, note card, 32-33

"The Jockey", 9

jockeys, topic, 8-11, 16-18
journals, 92-93

leaders, *see* school leaders
Letters and Science Scholars' Lounge, topic, 24, 43-44, 53
level of confidence, 126-127
liberal, political (table), 118-119; religious, 23
librarian, 29, 32
list of references, 81-83; *see also* bibliography
"locate" information, 28-30, 32, 83, 87
LSD, topic, 24-25

McCullers, Carson, 9

marginal, 118
marijuana use, 25, 73, 114-118
marriage patterns, *see* co-ed dorms
Martian, 38
mean, 61, 107, 127-128, 130; *see also* median, mode
median, 61, 107; *see also* mean, mode
medical expenses, *see* preliminary table
Mills, C. Wright, 3-4
misrepresentation, *see* ethics
mode, 61, 107; *see also* mean, median
Mort, *see* Uncle Mort
"my", writing, 71
"My Old Man", 9

negative findings, 53-54
Negro, *see* black race
neutral findings, 53
noncontinuous data, 121-122, 125; *see also* variable
nonrespondents, 40
nonwhites, income, 106-108
note cards, 32-33, 53-54, 83, 87; examples, 88-90

Sociological Abstracts, 2, 29
sociological imagination, 3-4
sociological perspective, 2
Sources of Information in the Social Sciences, 29, 32
special terms, *see* definition of terms
specific question, *see* structured question
specification, variable, 59
sports cars, topic, 55, 60-61
spurious relationship, 57
stack access, 31
standard deviation, 127-130
Statistical Abstracts of the United States, 106, 108, 111
statistics, association, 56-59, 120; average, 61, 120-121; average deviation, 128-129; basketball, 104; calculator, 118, 121; central tendency, 61; chi-square, 121-127; coefficient of correlation, 127-132; continuous data, 121, 125, 128; dependent variable, 56; drawing conclusions, 62, 123; expected frequency, 123-126; explanation, 58-59; frequency distribution, 60; further reference, 132-133; independent variable, 56; interpretation, 58-59; level of confidence, 126-127; marginal, 118; mean, 61, 107, 127-128, 130; median, 61, 107; mode, 61, 107; noncontinuous data, 121-122, 125; observed frequency, 123, 125-126; percent, 60, 109-111, 118-119, 121; probability, 127, 132; ratio, 60-61, raw numbers, 120, 122; specification, 59; spurious relationship, 57; standard deviation, 127-130; *Statistical Abstracts of the United States,* 106, 108, 111
stores, topic, 2
structured question, 41-42, 44
summary, library research, 27, 30, 32; table, 108
summary fever, 27; *see also* book report syndrome

survey, *see* preliminary research
suspended judgment, 70

table, basketball, 104; Bureau of the Census; "Personal Consumption Expenditures, by Product: 1950 to 1972", 109-111, 113; "Median Income in Constant (1973) Dollars of Families and Individuals by Race: 1947 to 1973", 106-107; "Wife's Contribution to Family Income — Families with Husband and Wife Working, by Race of Husband: 1959 and 1972", 107-108; numbering, 117, 119; preliminary, 112-113; text examples, "College Control of Sex, by Marijuana Use", 115; "Depression, by Marijuana Use", 114, 116; "Depression, by Marijuana Use and Sex", 117; "Influence of Political Ideology upon Attitudes Towards the Legalization of Marijuana", 118; "Personal Consumption Expenditures" (preliminary), 113; titling, 119; stock, 104; working, 123
tabulation sheets, *see* coding
tally, *see* coding
tape recorder, interview, 47
Techniques of Attitude Scale Construction, 100
tentative thesis, 22, 28, 54
terms, special, *see* defining terms
textual documentation, 80-81, 83; further reference, 83-84; *see also* footnote
theft, topic, 122-126, 129-132; *see also* green, red
topic drift, 14
topics, abortion, 8, 14-15, 37; artists, 35-37, 48; blacks, employees, 101; family life, 62, 106-108; buying habits, 54; cocktail waitresses, 96-97; co-ed dorms, 12-14; cheating, 41-42, 72; diets, 38-39; discrimination on campus, 95-96; dress, 3; drinking, 18-22, 56,

Index